CW00497086

Walking on Holy Ground

Walking on Holy Ground

A Pilgrimage on the Via Francigena
and the Western Front, from London to Laon

NICK DUNNE

© Nick Dunne, 2022

Published by Som Tam Books

All rights reserved. No part of this book may be reproduced, adapted, stored in a retrieval system or transmitted by any means, electronic, mechanical, photocopying, or otherwise without the prior written permission of the author.

The rights of Nick Dunne to be identified as the author of this work have been asserted in accordance with the Copyright, Designs and Patents Act 1988.

A CIP catalogue record for this book is available from the British Library.

ISBN 978-1-7396199-0-9

Book layout and cover design by Clare Brayshaw

Prepared and printed by:

York Publishing Services Ltd
64 Hallfield Road
Layerthorpe
York YO31 7ZQ

Tel: 01904 431213

Website: www.yps-publishing.co.uk

For Private Albert Bassett and Private Henry Dadd
who walked these paths before us

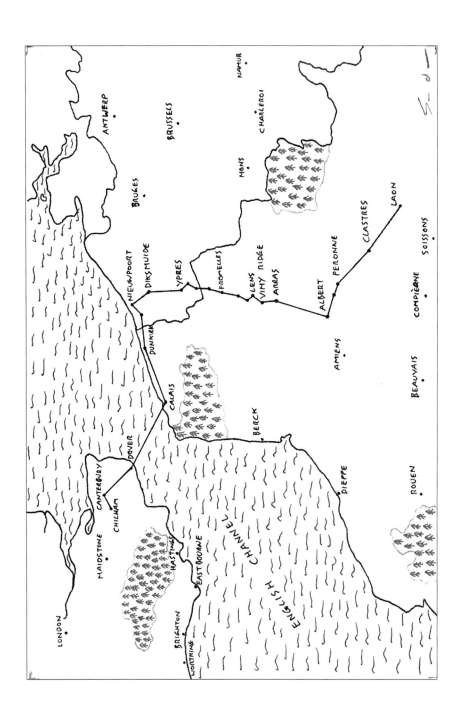

Contents

Acknowledgements

When I started this journey, I did not fully know its purpose, nor where it would lead. Now, as I finish this account of the first stage of our walk, the world is in lockdown. The coronavirus pandemic has changed our lives in ways no one could have imagined just a few months ago. The places we have walked through, even in our own country, are currently off-limits and, having reached Siena in 2019, we now wonder when, if ever, we might complete that final leg to Rome.

But the change has brought blessings too. Confined to Tooting in south London, we have discovered new footpaths on our morning walks and been rewarded with fresh insights into the parks and Common we thought we knew so well. Lockdown has given time to finish this work and it has inspired our son, Sam, to research family history. Family members have responded well to his enthusiasm, which encourages me to hope that they will enjoy this book too.

There are many people to thank, for many reasons. Firstly, our companions and hosts on the journey, all of whom have enriched our experience and helped make it memorable. Special thanks to Rev. Julia Butterworth, Stijn Butaye and Anne Walsh for sharing their stories with me. My thanks to Bernard Dive, Caroline Knight and the many friends who read early drafts of the book and encouraged me to consider publication. I'm very grateful to Chris Graham for proofreading the final version and saving me from some embarrassing errors and to the team at York Publishing Services for their support in bringing this book to publication. Special thanks to Tom Dunne for designing our route map, Chris Morgan for his companionship and guidance on the battlefields of the Great War and to his mother Eugenie (Jean) Morgan and cousin Gordon Dadd for their memories of Henry Dadd. Thanks too to Albert Bassett's daughters,

Joan Richmond and Nen Billings, and to Nen's husband Bill for their memories and extensive research into Albert Bassett's war-time service. Fiona and I are also grateful for the multilingual skills of Christian Franceschi who found us accommodation on the pilgrimage in small, wonderful places where English was not spoken.

I have made every effort to trace and acknowledge the owners and sources of material used in this book and my thanks to the many publishers who have given their permission to quote from their books and websites. Thanks also to the many free online sources, especially Wikipedia, that have enabled me to deepen my knowledge of the people, places and events that engaged me on the journey. I promise that I have made my donations when asked! My apologies for any failures or errors which, if brought to my attention, I will do my best to correct in future editions. All photographs were taken either by myself or by Fiona.

My final thanks are for Fiona, *le pèlerin avec un parapluie*, my perfect walking companion. Your patience with me, your resilience and wise judgement were all tested at times on the journey, but never faltered. For all our walks to come, I hope that, in the words of the song writer Leonard Cohen, "our steps will always rhyme". [1]

Nick Dunne
May 2020, Tooting Bec, London
somtambooks@btinternet.com

* * *

1. From "Hey That's No Way to Say Goodbye", on the album *Songs of Leonard Cohen* released by Columbia Records, 1967.

In Search of a Way

Preface: In Search of a Way

October 2013, Balham, South London

It is over 35 years since the idea of walking to Rome was first planted in my mind.

In 1978 I was about to move from Scotland to start work in London when I heard that a Jesuit priest, Fr Gerry W Hughes, had just published a book about his great walk to Rome. Fr Gerry had been a very influential figure at Glasgow University's Catholic Chaplaincy in Turnbull Hall. My friend Kevin Tayler had known him well, joining some of the long walks Fr Gerry would lead in the hills and countryside around the city. Fr Gerry was just completing his time at the Chaplaincy when I started attending Sunday evening Mass there with Kevin. The music at Turnbull Hall was excellent, the sermons stimulating and the discussions with friends over a beer afterwards were lively and challenging. I began to feel that religion could be exciting – it could be an adventure.

I was keen to read about Fr Gerry's great expedition but, for some reason or other, his book was hard to find in Edinburgh where I had been studying. I therefore asked my sister, Philippa, who was living in London, to track down a copy for me. Like many siblings, our lives were going in different directions. Two years younger than me, she had joined Rev Sun Myung Moon's Unification Church, which was generally known as "The Moonies" and had travelled widely with them around the world. Now she had a regular job in London working in the big Lloyds Bank building at Blackfriars Bridge. I was about to start my first job as a social worker helping homeless alcoholics in south London. It was an idealistic and a highly charged political time. In my eyes, she was moving to the Right, as I was moving to the Left and I was more than happy to have hard edged arguments with her about "the evils of capitalism". The 1970s were like that. Looking back, such debates produced very little wisdom for the upset they caused and I am so pleased that our friendship survived them.

We arranged to meet one evening at a pub by the river close to where she worked. The Doggett's Coat and Badge was a modern, multilevel glass and concrete construction that took its name from the prize given to the winner of the oldest rowing race in the world.[1] I have only ever been back to the pub once or twice since then but whenever I pass it, I do so with a feeling of affection born on that evening.

Despite our differences, Philippa and I had a very warm and happy session together. She'd found the book and I took it gratefully, eager to read of Fr Gerry's adventures. The title was *In Search of a Way – two journeys of discovery*.[2] The two journeys were his walk from Weybridge in Surrey to Rome in 1975, and his own personal spiritual journey reflecting on eight sometimes controversial years as chaplain at Glasgow University. During those years, conflict with Church authorities and challenges from sceptical, sometimes angry students had shaken the foundations of his life as a middle-aged Roman Catholic priest. I looked forward to finding in his journey some answers to my own doubts and questions about the Faith I'd been brought up in.

I'm now older than Fr Gerry was when he undertook his walk but I feel that I could achieve a similar journey, not as he did in one big trek over ten weeks, but in stages, long and short, as life, loves and responsibilities allow. However, in contemplating such a journey I hear the gentle Scottish voice of my school physics teacher, "Wee Charlie" asking, "Well, what's it all bloomin' well for?"

Wee Charlie was the nickname we gave to Mr McCloskey because he was short in stature and looked like the TV comedian Charlie Drake. After telling us how to conduct an experiment demonstrating, for example, wave theory or some principle of electromagnetism, Mr McCloskey would finish with his catchphrase question. "Well, what's it all bloomin' well for?" he'd ask his perplexed class before going on to reveal the hidden purpose of the exercise.

So, to answer Wee Charlie's question, I hope that this journey and the notes that arise from it may put some perspective on the years I have been privileged to live. I hope it will help me be grateful for the many blessings I have received and prepare me for the years that are still left to come.

By following the pilgrimage route between Canterbury and Rome, I will travel over holy ground. I hope that the structure and purpose of this journey will help me gather together those memories, insights, thoughts, questions (and some answers) that have perplexed and fascinated me over the years. In that sense, it will be a faith journey too, an exploration of not only the sacred places I travel through but also the holy ground that I carry within me.

Since reading Fr Gerry's book, I have walked whenever I could on long distance routes such as the Cotswold and West Highland Ways and shorter expeditions in the Surrey Hills and along the North Downs. Trips to the supermarket are given a hint of adventure as I shoulder an empty rucksack and imagine I am setting off again along footpaths less travelled. My wife Fiona and I have walked the final 100km of the popular pilgrim route to Santiago de Compostela, but it was a cautious journey. I was awaiting medical treatment for heart arrhythmia and had a pulse rate of 140, so we had our bags transported and we kept the daily distances short. Happily, I'm fully recovered and it is the Via Francigena that now holds my imagination. Volume 1 of Alison Raju's excellent, well researched pocket guide to the 1,900 km route has recently been published[3] and I have read and reread this to plan how I might make the journey.

Fr Gerry plotted his own course across the Continent in as straight a line as possible. He sailed from Newhaven to Dieppe, then passed through Paris, Grenoble, Genoa and Pisa before joining the traditional pilgrim route to Rome at Lucca. Much of his journey was along main roads so, whilst it is tempting to follow exactly in his footsteps, the Via Francigena is a far better option.

The route follows that taken in AD 990 by Sigeric, Archbishop of Canterbury, on his journey to and from Rome where he received his seal of office from the pope. Even before Sigeric's journey, travellers from Britain had used this route for centuries. From Calais they would go through Arras, Reims, Besançon and Lausanne to cross the Alps by the Great St Bernard Pass. From there, the way descended through Aosta, Piacenza and Lucca, before its final leg through Tuscany to Rome. It was a long and arduous journey, but when Sigeric reached his destination he only spent three days in the city. This was just long enough for him to receive his *pallium* from the Pope and to visit no less than 23 churches – a typically focused itinerary for the man who became known as Sigeric the Serious.[4] As they left, Sigeric asked his secretary to record the overnight stops they made on their way back to Canterbury, and this is the inspiration for the Via Francigena today.

In France, around Arras, the Via Francigena follows the line of the Great War's Western Front. Whilst I have visited many of its cemeteries and battlefields[5] I have never continuously walked the length of the Front itself. I have therefore decided to take this opportunity to detour north and walk the old battle lines from where they begin at the Belgian coast until they join the Via Francigena at Arras.

Therefore, instead of turning right out of Calais, I will turn left to begin my continental walk at the beaches of Dunkirk. Here, it could be argued, the First World War played out its final chapter when, in 1940, German forces finally captured the coastal ports that had been their target in 1914. From Dunkirk, I will walk north-east to where the Western Front reached the sea at the Belgian town of Nieuport, before following the trench lines south through Dixmude, Ypres and Messines to re-enter France at Armentières. A second expedition will take me to Loos, Arras and the Somme, before leaving the British section of the Front and following the Via Francigena through the unfamiliar French battlefields from Péronne towards the Chemin des Dames. I will finish this part of the walk over 300km from Canterbury at the medieval town of Laon and its famous Gothic cathedral.

The first 30km section, from Canterbury to the coast at Dover will, I hope, happen next weekend with Fiona and other friends. However, I do not know when the next section will be, let alone when our journey might conclude in Rome. That's part of the adventure. The walk will be a thread through whatever life brings us in the months and years to come.

In Search of a Way was very successful and, in the years that followed, Fr Gerry became a well-known author. I met him again in October 1996 when he was giving a one-day retreat at Worth Abbey in West Sussex. During the lunch break, Kevin Tayler and I chatted with him about the Glasgow University days. I had brought the book that Philippa had given me and he was delighted to see it. "I've not seen one of these first editions for a long time," he said as he signed it. I have it with me now as I write this and I see how apt his dedication was. On the fly-leaf he has written: *"For Nick, with best wishes for your own journey, Gerry Hughes."*

* * *

1. Thomas Doggett was a successful Irish actor. In 1715, he decided to celebrate King George's accession to the throne by awarding the prize to the winner of a rowing race along the Thames from London Bridge to Chelsea. The race still takes place each year.
2. *In Search of a Way*, by Fr Gerard W Hughes SJ, first published by E J Dwyer 1978, republished by Darton, Longman & Todd, 1986.
3. *Via Francigena, Pilgrim Trail Canterbury to Rome Volume 1*, by Alison Raju, published by Cicerone 2011.
4. An Archbishop's seal of office was the pallium, a narrow band of white wool decorated with six black crosses. Worn looped over the neck and shoulders, the ends fall to front and back and create its distinctive Y shape. Sigeric's epithet "The Serious" may have arisen as an acknowledgement of his diligent study, or from the Latin translation of his name.
5. This was to research members of my parish church who had been killed during the Great War. Their story is told in *A Parish in Wartime*, by Nick Dunne and John Pontifex, 2014, published by St Anselm's Church, Tooting Bec www.stanselmstbec.org

Ceramics by Adam Kossowski, at The Friars, Aylesford.

*"Initially, I thought them rather crude and gaudy, but, over many visits,
I have become very fond of their distinctive character."*

Part One – April 2014

South London, Rochester, Aylesford, Chilham, Canterbury, Dover, Calais, Dunkirk, Veunes, Nieuport, Ypres, Messines, Armentières

"The great doors of Canterbury Cathedral's Christ Church gate were closed and we had to ring the bell. As we waited, we admired a scallop shell, the pilgrims' symbol, carved into the door's ancient timbers."

CHAPTER ONE

In the Company of Good Friends

South London, Rochester, Aylesford, Chilham, Canterbury

The best laid plans…

Heavy rain forced us to abandon the idea of walking from Canterbury in October. It had been a frustrating weekend. I was keen to get going, but opinion was divided within the group of walkers gathering for that day. Reluctantly, I had conceded that, in the circumstances, a postponement was probably wise. However, I realised that if this walk was to happen I could not afford the complexity of involving too many walking companions.

The revised plan was to start at the village of Chilham, just outside of Canterbury. The path would take us along the final miles of the Pilgrims' Way, the ancient road to Becket's shrine from Winchester, and probably the best-known walking pilgrims' route in England. This decision confirmed that my journey to Rome was, in fact, the continuation of a pilgrimage I had started in 2002 when I had walked to Canterbury from the front door of my home in south London.

I had been working for many years with a charity that provided emergency accommodation and supported housing for street homeless men, many of whom had chronic alcohol and mental health problems. When we merged with another charity, it was time for me to make a change and I took voluntary redundancy. Although I did not know what my next job would be, I trusted that things would work out. Meanwhile, I had the rare opportunity of a block of uncommitted time and I decided to use it to explore pilgrim places close to home and close to my heart.

For centuries, the old Roman road of Stane Street had connected London Bridge and Chichester. Now, as the busy A24, it passed very near to our home in Tooting Bec so I decided to follow the original route as closely as possible as far as Dorking. There Stane Street crossed the Pilgrims' Way to continue south to the coast. I would leave the Roman road at Dorking to go east and follow the path to Canterbury.

I'd managed to persuade my 14 year old son, Tom, to accompany me to Dorking so, early one December morning we walked out of our front door in Tooting Bec, turned right and tracked the old Roman way. Over the next two days, the path took us through south London's suburban sprawl, past the few remaining ruins of St Thomas Becket's old school at Merton Abbey and the site of Queen Elizabeth I's palace at Nonsuch Park until, following a final series of footpaths through woods, we reached Dorking.

Tom then left me to continue my journey alone. I still had family duties to perform at night. Tom and his younger brother Sam had school to prepare for and homework to supervise and, with no job secured, I needed to be economical with my budget. So, after each day's walking I would take the train home and then reverse the journey next day to resume my expedition. This method of "daily commutes" to different sections of the North Downs Way was an ideal compromise. Having saved on the cost of overnight accommodation, I could enjoy each morning sitting on empty trains going in the opposite direction to those packed with glum, city bound passengers.

At Dorking, I climbed Box Hill and then followed the trail east, past Otford and Wrotham, until I eventually reached Rochester on the Medway river. Here the Romans had built their bridge, Gundulf the Norman had built his castle and cathedral and England's great writer, Charles Dickens, had hoped to be buried.

* * *

I was born not far from Rochester in an upstairs room of a corner shop on Featherby Road in Gillingham. It was the 1950s and, although my parents were living in a flat in London's West Kensington, Mum had returned to her parents' home to give birth to me whilst Dad went to work each day as usual. There were no special concessions in those days to enable fathers to attend the birth of their children.

Nearly two years later, the same arrangements were made when my sister, Philippa, was born. I remember standing at the foot of the stairs in Featherby Road and being told by my grandmother, Nana, that I couldn't go upstairs yet. It was unusual for Nana to stop me from going to see Mum, so I knew something important was happening but I didn't understand what. That feeling of bemusement has remained with me and it is my first conscious memory.

During the 1980s, Mum composed a brief and very well written memoir to introduce the jumble of loose family photographs she was ordering into albums. She recorded that my birth, and that of my sister, *were both 'home' confinements... I was attended by Nurse Maisie who attended my sister [Anne's] birth in 1940, and Dr Roffey who had attended my birth [in 1928]. Full circle."*

Gillingham is one of the string of towns that include Rochester, Chatham, Strood and Rainham that merge into one along the river Medway. Chatham is the focus. For 400 years it was an important Naval dockyard, a hub of employment and industry that dominated this part of north Kent until it finally closed in 1984.

My Nana, Dorothy Cookney, was a London girl, one of a family of 10. At the age of 12, her father had woken her one September night in 1916 to see a German airship on fire in the night sky. German airships had been bombing the city for over a year and these terrifying monster machines had seemed unstoppable. This was the first one to be shot down and thousands of Londoners came onto the streets that night to watch it falling slowly to earth and crash at Cuffley in the Hertfordshire countryside.

Many years later, in 1927, Dorothy was living in Chatham with an older brother, Cyril, when she met a sailor of the Royal Navy, Leonard Kempster. It was a brief courtship, just a few weeks she told me, and they were married that same year. Perhaps it was in the stars. Although four years separated them in age, they both shared the same May birthday.

Len had joined the Navy aged 15 and went on to serve in both world wars. We have a photograph of him as a young lad, slim and proud in his new Navy uniform. However, Len's looks changed over the years to his retirement at the age of 45. When he went to hand in his uniform and collect a new civilian suit from the Navy, the storeman cast a practiced eye over Len's height and shape before announcing his conclusion. "Short and portly," he called to his colleague, who then selected appropriate jacket and trousers for Len to wear in his new life.

To prepare for "civvie street", the Navy gave Len a basic training in gents' hairdressing. So, whilst his wife ran the confectionery side of the business, Len adapted half of the shop at Featherby Road into a barber's from where, my Mum wrote, he performed *"a passable short, back and sides"* for his customers.

In temperament, Len was a worrier. Mum remembered: *"If there was a train to be caught, he always arrived at the station in time to miss the previous one! Nevertheless, he had a wry sense of humour and like me appreciated the unconscious rather than the obvious comedy of life."*

I have only one memory of Grandad Len and that was of being allowed to sit up in bed with him to watch television. This was a great privilege and I enjoyed sitting beside him under the blankets. However, I did not realise that it was illness that confined him there so early in the day. He died in 1959 at the relatively young age of 59.

Although I hardly knew him, I was very aware of my Grandad's place in history. On our bookshelf at home there was a thick, grandly bound book entitled *The National Roll of the Great War 1914–1918, Section V, Luton*. I still have it and I look now at its 401 pages of names and brief service histories, each page with two columns, nine names to a column. The scale of the record is awesome and there, on page 202, is my Grandad's name and a brief summary of his service history:

> "He volunteered in 1915, and after his training was engaged in important and hazardous duties in His Majesty's destroyers and cruisers. His vessel was in action in the Dardanelles, and cruised in the Mediterranean Sea, and off the coasts of India and Turkey. "H.M.S. Weymouth" in which he was serving, was torpedoed, but he was saved, and in 1920 was still with his ship off the coast of Ireland. He holds the 1914–15 Star, and the General Service and Victory Medals."

The torpedo attack, by the Austrian submarine U28, took place on October 2, 1918. I have a photograph taken after the *Weymouth* had staggered safely into harbour. There is a huge hole in its stern and its rear deck is twisted and crumpled as if torn apart by a giant can opener. It is a miracle that the ship survived. Eight seamen are gathered informally at the rail close to the damage. They are too small and out of focus to identify but, of course, I am tempted to wonder if I am looking at my young Grandad shaken but proud after his ordeal by fire.

* * *

Rochester's cathedral has claim to be the second oldest in England. Founded in AD 604, work began in 1080 to replace the crumbling Saxon structure with a grand cathedral worthy of the new Norman regime. The building that is treasured today still contains large sections of the original work of its creator, Gundulf, architect and monk from the Abbey at Bec. A close friend of St Anselm, Gundulf followed King William from Normandy to build not only Rochester's cathedral, but also the castle opposite and the White Tower which still gleams from the centre of the famous Tower of London.

In Rochester Cathedral, I climbed the steps and lit a candle at the site of the shrine to St William of Perth. William was a successful baker who, after a wild youth, had committed himself to the Christian faith. He would attend Mass every day and he would always set aside every tenth loaf he baked to be given to the poor.

One morning, before dawn, William found a baby abandoned at the door of the church. He adopted the child, named him David and taught him his trade. When he decided to make a pilgrimage to the Holy Land, William invited David to join him. The pair had already travelled nearly 500 miles when, in 1201, they decided to rest for a while in Rochester. They stayed in the city for three days before resuming their journey along the Roman road towards Maidstone. Soon, David suggested that they take a shortcut. The path led them into a quiet place out of sight of the road and there, for whatever cruel reason, David decided to rob his father. He knocked William to the ground and cut his throat.

It was a while before William's body was found. A mentally disturbed woman discovered him lying on the ground. Tenderly, she placed a garland of honeysuckle, first on William's head and then on her own. As she did this, the madness left her. She ran to the city to tell the monks and they came to take William's body and bury him in the Cathedral. The healing of the madwoman was the first of many miracles and William was declared a saint in 1256. William's cult grew, a chapel was built at the scene of his murder and his Cathedral shrine became a focus of pilgrimage second only to that of Thomas Becket at Canterbury.

The Reformation destroyed the shrine and William's relics were lost. However, the deep recesses worn in the stone steps still testify to the thousands of feet that have come this way to pay tribute to the murdered pilgrim. The story does not say what happened to David and whether he ever paid for his crime. Perhaps there was some form of reconciliation because, despite David's treachery, William of Perth became the patron saint of adopted children. He is not well known now, but the few candles that burn at the site of his shrine tell us he is not entirely forgotten.

* * *

Heading south along the river bank I passed the remains of jetties where, in years gone by, flying boats were serviced and repaired. My Mum had told me how after the Second World War she used to see dozens of RAF Sunderlands riding at anchor. "It was a wonderful sight," she said.

Some 12 kilometres or so further on, I left the North Downs Way and dropped from the ridge to rejoin the Medway's riverbank and stay a night at the Way's most authentic pilgrimage site, the Carmelite Friars at Aylesford.

Founded in 1242, the Carmelite community had welcomed Canterbury pilgrims for nearly 300 years. After its dissolution in 1538, the friary became a private manor house until, in 1949, the Carmelites returned to restore the medieval buildings and create a new shrine. To celebrate the restoration, Bordeaux Cathedral donated part of the skull of St Simon Stock, an English Carmelite who had lived in the Aylesford community during the 13th century. A special reliquary was needed to house the saint's relic and so a Polish artist, Adam Kossowski, was chosen to create it.

Kossowski had been seized when the Soviets invaded Poland in 1939 and forced to work in Russian labour camps. The conditions were terrible and the young man began to pray. Many years later he told an interviewer,

"When I was so deep in this calamity and nearly dead, I promised myself that if I came out of this subhuman land, I would tender my thanks to God. I hesitate to call it a vow, it was rather a promise to myself but later I used to think that it was my obligation."[1]

When Germany turned on its Soviet ally and invaded in 1941, Stalin quickly negotiated terms for Britain and America to come to his aid. One of the conditions of the alliance was that Poles held in captivity were to be freed. Kossowski was released and eventually in 1943 joined other Polish exiles in London. Here his artistic skills flourished and his first major commission came from Aylesford's Carmelites in 1950. Kossowski continued to work with the Carmelite community for over 20 years and his ceramics and paintings can be found in every chapel at the Friars.

Initially, I thought them rather crude and gaudy but, over many visits, I have become very fond of their distinctive character. They reflect the depth of his relationship with the Friars, and his gratitude for having survived the "subhuman land" of the Gulag. They are works of love and, through them, the Friars is as much a shrine to his hope and thanksgiving as it is to the bones of St Simon Stock.

* * *

In many respects, the Friars brought my wife Fiona and me together. We were already colleagues at the Alcoholics Recovery Project (ARP), a charity which helped single and street homeless men and women stop drinking and rebuild their lives. It was challenging work, and we had pooled our experience to write a manual of discussion group topics to help participants reflect on how to turn a fragile time "off the bottle" into a robust sobriety upon which to build a new life.[2] One year, the Friars was chosen to be the venue for ARP's winter staff conference. The sound of the Angelus being broadcast over loud speakers at noon raised a few eyebrows amongst our agnostic colleagues gathered around the flipcharts, but the very reasonable prices and the beautiful location beside the Medway river more than compensated for any cultural discomfort.

The religious significance of this Carmelite retreat house did not interest us at that time, but the ancient architecture was impressive. This was particularly true of the great Pilgrims' Hall. Now used as a dining room for visitors, this huge barn of a building dates from medieval times and had, for generations, welcomed those who were on their way to St Thomas' Shrine in Canterbury. Huge oak beams supported the long sloping roof above our heads, with galleries on two levels creating quiet spaces for reading and study that were apart from, but still connected to the communality of shared meals taking place below. Here I summoned up the courage to ask Fiona out on her birthday which was a few days later. I expected her diary to be already fully booked but, to my delight she accepted and the evening was ours to spend together.

We started with a trip to the cinema to see Indiana Jones' wonderful adventures in *Raiders of the Lost Ark*. From there, we followed our friend Ron Kerr's recommendation to a Malaysian restaurant in a Soho side street. This would be our first experience of such cuisine. As we settled at our table we noticed the sound of a heavy disco beat pulsing through the walls. We remembered then that Ron had warned us the building next door to the restaurant was a brothel.

We enjoyed an excellent evening, despite the fact that Fiona was struggling with a heavy cold. Towards the end of the meal she realised that she had run out of tissues. We asked the waiter if he had any. "Of course," he said. Then, to our surprise, he tore off a large piece of our paper tablecloth and, with a flourish and a smile, gallantly presented it to Fiona. We thanked him and the crisis was averted. It remains to this day one of the most creative examples of "customer care" we have ever come across.

That winter's night was relatively mild, so we walked together around St James' Park. The Virginia creeper covering the walls of the wartime fortress near Admiralty Arch had turned red, transforming the ugly building into something quite beautiful. In the soft street lights, the rich colour glowed magically and we realised our lives were entering a new and wonderful dimension.

Since then, I have been back to the Friars on many occasions and it is one of my favourite places to withdraw, reflect and appreciate life and the blessings I have. Each time I return, I recall that gamble I took to risk rejection back then in 1981 and I still find, absorbed in the medieval timbers, the happiness I felt when she said "yes".

* * *

The Via Francigena ("the way through France") is the natural extension of England's Pilgrims' Way and on this fine spring day in April 2014 we were at last underway.

Fiona and I took the 10.19 am train from London Bridge and 90 minutes later we were in the picture postcard village of Chilham with its castle, its church and its ancient timber-framed buildings.

We found seats outside Shelly's Tea Rooms on the village square and drank coffee whilst we planned the day's walking. Across the road by the castle gates, two life-size medieval pilgrims sculpted from an old oak tree marked a sign which told us it was seven miles to Canterbury along this, the last stage of the Pilgrims' Way.

Our guidebook to the North Downs Way[3] suggested that this small village might in fact have a had a bigger role in England's Christian history than we were aware of. It reported that Chilham's parish church of St Mary had been founded in AD 182 by King Lucius, the first Christian King of England. In the churchyard, an old yew tree dated to around AD 690 confirmed the village's ancient origins. Furthermore, there were rumours that, after the Reformation had destroyed his shrine in Canterbury Cathedral, the bones of St Augustine had been reburied in or near the village church. A very old marble sarcophagus with a cross carved into its lid had been found in St Mary's and some thought it could have held St Augustine's remains.

Augustine was an Italian monk who, in AD 596, was chosen by Pope Gregory the Great to leave his monastery in Rome and lead a mission to evangelise the Anglo-Saxons in this part of England. It was a tough challenge and, by the time the monks had reached Gaul, Augustine and his followers were having second thoughts. They asked permission to turn back, but Pope Gregory encouraged them to continue, strengthening the size of the party and promoting Augustine to Bishop. So, in 597, Augustine together with 40 monks and priests landed at Ebbsfleet on the Kent coast. Today, the Kent coastline takes a different course and the site of Augustine's landing is actually half a mile or so inland, west of Ramsgate. A Victorian stone cross in a quiet field marks the place where Christianity returned to this part of the British Isles.

By the time that Augustine died in 604 he had successfully converted the powerful King Ethelbert to Christianity and established Canterbury as the base from which further missions could spread throughout the country. When the sarcophagus at Chilham was found in 1860 local hopes were raised that it would contain Augustine's sacred relics. If it was true, Chilham could claim to be an important pilgrimage site in its own right.

We found the stone sarcophagus tucked into the north east corner of St Mary's church. Made of prized Purbeck marble, the worn but elaborately carved cross on its lid was a sure sign that the tomb had been created for someone of importance. A nearby notice told us how, in 1948, local historians had decided to open the sarcophagus to discover the truth. With respect and reverence, the great slab with its carved cross had been levered up and slid open. As torches probed the interior of the tomb, those gathered round held their breath in expectation. What they discovered did indeed surprise them, but not in the way they had hoped. There were no bones inside, only pieces of paper. These were the records of no fewer than three previous examinations, in 1883, 1904 and 1914. On each occasion, the results were the same. The tomb was completely empty.

As if to add to the disappointment, another notice informed us that the identity of King Lucius and his leading role in bringing Christianity to Britain is far from certain. The story is probably the result of a typo error in a 6th Century manuscript.[4] Good, solid scholarship had brought our flights of fancy right down to earth.

We left the church and followed the path along the side of the churchyard down to the road. There was much to reflect on. Christianity claims solid, historical foundations. Jesus' life, death and, most importantly, his Resurrection are not presented as myths or legends but tangible events in history involving real people who lived 2,000 years ago. This can be tough for the critical mind to accept. People do not "rise from the dead" no matter how clever or good they are. For long periods of my life I have been troubled that all this religious edifice might be founded on nothing more than a mistake, a typo error like that of the story of King Lucius. Stories of faith have to be scrutinised for their historical authenticity as well as for the wisdom they may convey. It would have been a good story to find a little known but genuine place of pilgrimage in Chilham. As it turned out, our visit reminded us just how difficult the historical search can be.

* * *

Crossing the road, we were soon absorbed in a peaceful landscape of close, folding hills, bluebell woods and energetic birdsong. The low cloud brought a rich stillness in the quiet, hazy grey atmosphere. Beyond the village of Old Wives Lees, we came upon huge orchards of apple trees. Recent winds had thinned their pink and white blossom but their colour and the petals' intricate beauty were still vibrant.

The route dropped down through a colony of caravans parked beside a farm. It was too early in the year for the migrant workers who come and live here during the harvest season, so most of the caravans were empty. We paused to chat with a man who spoke perfect English with an Eastern European accent. He told us that the Bramley apples would be ready in six months' time and he encouraged us to visit again then. Past Chartham Hatch, a community orchard invited walkers to help themselves to apples from the trees beside the path but, alas, there were none to pick this early in the year.

A little further on we reached the site of Bigbury Camp, an ancient settlement where, in 54 BC, it is believed Julius Caesar and his army fought a battle with local tribes. Here the path slipped down into a great hollow within the wood, drawing us into the mystery of the place. The clouds were low and solid in the sky and there was no breeze to disturb the day's stillness. We were the only people there. As we walked on, the slopes to our right, cleared of trees, revealed lines of ditches and flat plateaux that had been created over 2,000 years ago. Our map showed a busy dual carriageway, the A2, less than half a kilometre away but we couldn't hear a sound of any traffic. All we could hear was birdsong, and the faint intimations of an ancient past.

* * *

We had chosen our entry point into Canterbury carefully. I had read that the relics of a saint lay in the vault of a church close to one of the old city gates. Now, just outside the city's West Gate, St Dunstan's generous grass churchyard with its trees and bluebells gave us a final glimpse of the countryside before entering the city.

Two great men of history have each made their mark on St Dunstan's. The first of these, King Henry II, was on his own path of penance when he arrived at the church on July 8, 1174. By travelling in person to Canterbury, Henry had hoped to redeem himself for his part in the murder of its archbishop, his old friend Thomas Becket.

Relations between Henry and Thomas had soured almost as soon as the king appointed Becket as archbishop. Church and State were in a power struggle and, to Henry's dismay, his old friend proved to be a formidable adversary. In 1164, Thomas was charged with contempt of royal authority and fled to France. The Pope intervened and, in 1170, Becket was allowed to return from exile. However, almost immediately he reignited his dispute with Henry by excommunicating three of the king's most senior church officials. Henry was incensed and launched into a tirade against his former friend. His words changed the course of history. Looking at the courtiers around him, Henry is said to have demanded *"Who will rid me of this troublesome priest?"*[5]

Reginald FitzUrse, Hugh de Morville, William de Tracy and Richard le Bret took Henry's outburst as their mandate. They set off from the king's court near Bayeux in Normandy and planned their own solution to the king's challenge. Crossing the Channel, they met again at Saltwood Castle which stands to this day close to the coastal town of Hythe. There they were welcomed by fellow conspirators Ranulf and Robert de Broc and together they refined their plans to confront the Archbishop. On December 28, 1170, the six men journeyed together to Canterbury accompanied by a troop of men-at-arms. They quickly covered the 14 miles to the city where, on Tuesday December 29, the party had time to eat and drink with the Abbot of St Augustine's Abbey (another of Thomas' opponents) before confronting Becket in a room off the hall of the archbishop's palace. It was about 4.30 pm and the events leading up to Becket's murder are documented in incredible detail by an eyewitness, a Saxon monk named Edward Grim.[6]

Earlier that afternoon, Thomas had dined well and had drunk more than usual. He was in no mood to meekly accept the four knights' reports of the king's complaints against him. The argument spiralled, insults were exchanged and the knights, in a rage, stormed out into the garden. There they buckled on their swords before running into an orchard at the back of the palace to break into the staircase leading to Becket's bedroom.

Meanwhile, Becket was preparing for Vespers at 5 pm. Although he could hear the shouts of the armed soldiers outside, he and his attendants continued to make their way through the cloister into the Cathedral.

The four knights with their men-at-arms found Thomas Becket in the north transcept. There in that holy place, decorated for Christmas to celebrate the birth of the Prince of Peace, the final act was played out. First, to avoid committing sacrilege, the knights tried to drag Becket out of the Cathedral. The Archbishop resisted strongly, wrestling with the knights and their assistants and shouting abuse at them. Grabbing William de Tracy by his coat-of-mail, Becket hurled him to the stone pavement. FitzUrse wielded his sword but merely dislodged the Archbishop's cap. The Archbishop's attendant, Edward Grim, wrapped his arm in a cloak and brought it round Becket to protect him. Throwing his arm up, Grim parried a blow from De Tracy before a second brought Thomas to the ground. Richard le Bret struck next with such violence that his sword sliced off the top of Becket's skull. Finally, a lowly clerk who had joined the crowd assisting the knights, completed the butchery. Hugh Mauclerk planted his foot on Becket's neck and thrust his sword into his skull, scattering the brains in the spreading pool of blood. *"Let us go,"* he is reported to have said, *"the traitor is dead: he will rise no more."*

Reading these accounts, it seems that Becket's murder followed a familiar tragic pattern. It's a sequence, almost a ritualistic dance, that has been played out in bars and taverns across the centuries. It begins with heavy drinking that leads to an argument. There is an interval after one party leaves in bitter mood, then develops a new intensity when that person returns having armed themselves with gun or knife. There are more threats and taunts, before, inevitably, a fatal blow is struck. On reflection, you can see distinct stages, lines, where the episode could have ended but, instead, the conflict escalates with jibes and gestures, the protagonists winding themselves up to cross another line, to take one more step towards that most unnatural of deeds, the killing of another person.

When King Henry heard of the murder he shut himself up for three days, ate nothing except almonds and milk, donned sackcloth and ashes and frequently shouted out that he was not responsible for the crime. Becket's murder led to public outcry which refused to absolve the king from blame. Almost immediately, Becket's tomb became a focus of pilgrimage. Becket's blood was mixed with gallons of water and the famous Water of St Thomas distributed to those in poor health. Miraculous cures were soon attributed to his supernatural intervention and these were quickly investigated. In 1173, less than three years after his murder, Pope Alexander III officially canonised Becket, declaring the date of his death, December 29, as the Feast of St Thomas of Canterbury.

By 1174, King Henry had already done public penance. He'd repeatedly stated his innocence and made offers of restitution, but none of this had been enough to change the mood against him. Faced with mounting problems at home, he left his campaigns in Normandy and sailed for Southampton. Living on a penitential diet of bread and water, he rode to Canterbury, probably along the Pilgrims' Way. Arriving at the outskirts of the city on July 8, 1174, he entered St Dunstan's church where he stripped off his clothes and put on the hair shirt and woollen dress of a penitential pilgrim. Then, barefoot and cloaked against the rain, he walked on bleeding feet through Canterbury's streets to the Cathedral.

Reaching the north transcept, Henry fell to his knees and, with tears in his eyes, kissed the stone where Becket had collapsed. In the crypt he knelt groaning and weeping. Removing his cloak, he put his head and shoulders through the aperture in the veined marble tomb that encased Becket's sacred remains. Through this opening, pilgrims could touch the coffin and be close to St Thomas. Now, as if in the presence of the saint himself, the King of England was beaten. Every Bishop and Abbot present administered five strokes and every monk struck three times.

This was no trivial punishment. On returning to London, King Henry had to take to his sick bed to recover. It was, however, worth it. Henry finally received the absolution that he craved and his political fortunes improved. Ironically, St Thomas was credited as having a hand in the King's good fortune and thereafter the martyr-saint enjoyed the royal patronage.

This theme of reconciliation even extended to St Thomas' four executioners. The knights may, or may not, have factored it into their plans, but one of the principles that Becket had stood up for against the King's wishes was that laymen who murdered priests should only be tried by clerical courts. As a result, the maximum sentence that the four knights could receive was excommunication. Within two years, they were all back at the royal court, enjoying the king's company and prospering. However, there is evidence that one of them at least may have pondered the eternal implications of his part in Thomas' martyrdom. Not four years after the murder, William de Tracy, who had struck the first and second blows and who was now a very rich and powerful landowner, made over to Canterbury Cathedral the manor of Dockham in Devonshire *"for the love of God, and the salvation of his own soul and his ancestors, and for the love of the blessed Thomas Archbishop and Martyr."* De Tracy's bequest was to provide clothing and support for one monk to celebrate masses for the souls of the living and dead, especially for his own.[7]

* * *

St Dunstan's second great man of history is remembered by an inscribed stone tablet on the floor of its St Nicholas' chapel. This tablet marks the entrance to a sealed vault within which the head of St Thomas More lies buried.

I knew the headlines from the film *A Man for All Seasons*. Like Becket, Thomas More went from being a close friend and confidante of a king (Henry VIII) to being charged with treason. He refused to recognise Henry as the head of the Church of England and so was sentenced to be "hung, drawn and quartered". The information panels on the wall of St Dunstan's gave a detailed account of More's life, trial and death. Reading them, I was particularly struck by the compassionate, indeed humorous words More spoke to his judges, his executioner and, even, King Henry himself. One saying is particularly famous. As he approached his execution, More cleverly defined the integrity of his political and spiritual loyalties with the phrase *"I am the King's man, but God's first."* It summed up his clarity of thought and his gift with words.

I was relieved to read that, although there was no last-minute reprieve, Thomas' sentence was commuted to the mercifully swift "beheading". However, this act of clemency did not extend to respecting his mortal remains.

After his execution on Tower Hill, Thomas More's body was dumped in an unmarked grave in the chapel of St Peter ad Vincula within the walls of the Tower of London. His severed head was stuck on a pike and displayed at London Bridge. More's daughter, Margaret Roper, retrieved it and brought it to St Dunstan's where she placed it in her family vault.

The Roper family vault is normally kept sealed. However, when it was opened for maintenance some years ago, photographs were taken which show the remains of Thomas' skull resting in a niche behind a metal grill in the vault's wall.

More was proclaimed a martyr and saint by the Roman Catholic church in 1935 but the Church of England, whose establishment was at the centre of his dispute with Henry, took a little longer to decide his place in the sacred order of things. In 1980, Thomas More was included in the Church of England's list of "Saints and Heroes of the Christian Church" and is commemorated on the date of his execution, July 6, as a Reformation Martyr.

* * *

Fiona and I entered the city through the West Gate. We'd booked a room in the Canterbury Cathedral Lodge, a conference centre and hotel in the precincts of the cathedral itself. It felt a privileged place to be. Coming back from our evening meal in town, the great doors of the Christ Church gate were closed and we had to ring the bell. As we waited, we admired a scallop shell, the pilgrims' symbol, carved into the door's ancient timbers. After a few moments, the side door opened slowly. We showed our special pass (our hotel room ticket) to a uniformed security man and were graciously nodded into this secret world at the heart of the city. Fiona and I had the grounds and gardens to ourselves. The Cathedral itself was locked and dark but, through its great walls, there came the sound of organ music. Someone was having a last practice of the day.

* * *

1. "An Interview with Adam Kossowski, 1978 by Fr. Martin Sankey, O. Carm.", Adam Kossowski: Murals and Paintings, page 70. Quoted in https://en.wikipedia.org/wiki/Adam_Kossowski
2. It's Not Just Willpower – A practical guide to helping alcoholics by F Richmond and N Dunne, published by ARP, 1983.
3. The North Downs Way by Denis Herbstein, published by the Countryside Commission, HMSO 1982, page 120.
4. See https://en.wikipedia.org/wiki/Lucius_of_Britain for a summary of the debate.
5. https://en.wikipedia.org/wiki/Will_no_one_rid_me_of_this_turbulent_priest%3F has a summary of the historic source of this well-known phrase attributed to King Henry II.
6. See the account in The Pilgrims' Way by John Adair, © 1978. Reprinted by

kind permission of Thames & Hudson Ltd., London, pages 36, 37. See also, Howard Loxton's *Pilgrimage to Canterbury*, 1978, published by David and Charles. Edward Grim's detailed account is on pages 65–72 and referenced with the kind permission of the publishers.

7.   John Adair, *The Pilgrims' Way* page 38. The British Museum's 2021 exhibition "Thomas Becket: Murder and the Making of a Saint" provides additional insights into the fate of the four knights. Curators Lloyd de Beer and Naomi Speakman note that Henry barred the knights' male heirs from inheriting property and that the knights personally sought absolution for their crime from the Pope himself – perhaps travelling to Rome by the Via Francigena. The Pope commanded them to go on pilgrimage to the Holy Land and William de Tracy's request that the monks at Canterbury pray for his soul is recorded in a charter he issued from Cosenza, in the south of Italy. De Tracy, FitzUrse, de Morville and le Bret (whom the exhibition identifies as Brito) are believed to have all died either in Jerusalem or on the way there. https://blog.britishmuseum.org/who-killed-thomas-becket

Chilham's pilgrims

CHAPTER TWO

An Unexpected Blessing

Canterbury to Dover

I woke at 5 am the next morning, excited by having this special place to ourselves. Through the bedroom window, I could see dawn breaking behind the shadow of the great Cathedral. Strips of cloud, transformed into bands of gold against the emerging blue sky, carried the promise of a new day. The freshness of that early morning was filled with hope and expectation of the adventure to come.

Leaving the hotel, I walked to the walled garden where a blackbird was singing cheerfully. There I found the words of William Wilberforce, the great campaigner against slavery, inscribed on a stone monument. It was as if he were here with me, speaking for this moment:

"The day has been delightful. I was out before six and made the fields my oratory, the sun shining as bright and warm as at midsummer. I think my own devotions become more fervent when offered in this way amidst the general chorus with which all nature seems on such a morning to be swelling the song of praise and thanksgiving."

Wondrous as that early morning garden was, I was already anticipating our privileged access to that great and wondrous place of stone now towering above the trees.

I'd worked out many years ago that the best way to enjoy the majesty of great cathedrals is to go to their early morning service. Obvious as it may seem, very few people visit a holy place by actually "going to church".

Instead, their visit will most likely be shared with hundreds of other people jostling around the historic sights, reading guidebooks and inscriptions and taking countless photographs.

However, if you are prepared to skip breakfast and make your way as I have done through the silent early morning streets of great cities like London, York, Turin, Venice and even the Vatican itself you will share the vastness of a sacred space with just a handful of equally intrepid visitors and enjoy an experience to treasure. So it was that Fiona and I took our places alongside six other people in the small side chapel at the west end of Canterbury Cathedral and waited for the 8 am Eucharist to begin.

High on the wall above the altar were the names of each archbishop who had served Canterbury from Augustine's inauguration in AD 602 through Lanfranc's, Anselm's and Becket's to Justin Welby's in 2013. Unlike the parish church of Chilham, there was no doubting the historical authenticity of this place. The list of names and dates is unbroken and 1400 years are covered in just a couple of panels. It made me realise that what we think of as ancient history is, really, not so long ago. Indeed, by being part of this morning's Eucharist, we were contributing in a small way to the evolving spiritual history of this place.

With a few moments to go before 8 am, a balding, bespectacled middle-aged man wearing a smart-casual brown jacket over an open-necked shirt hurried into the chapel. He settled in a chair a few places to my left but then got up and began to make his way back to the chapel's entrance where there was a small pile of Order of Service booklets. However, before he reached them he realised that the clergy were already processing towards the chapel so, slightly flustered, he gave up his quest for a booklet and returned to his seat.

Fiona and I had our booklets and I made a mental note to offer him one if he seemed to be struggling at any time to follow the prayers. I might be a Roman Catholic but I'd been to a few Church of England services, so I wasn't a complete newcomer. I promised myself that I'd look after him if he needed anyone to "show him the ropes".

Before arriving in Canterbury I'd taken up an invitation on the Cathedral's website for pilgrims to receive a blessing at the start of their journey. The Canon Pastor promptly emailed me back to say that Rev Julia Butterworth was saying the morning Eucharist and that she would be happy to do this for us. Rev Julia had been very thoughtful, leaving a letter for us at the hotel confirming our arrangements and then warmly welcoming us as we ventured through the great doors and into that vast Cathedral nave. Now, fully robed, she took her place at the altar.

In the years since the great debate on women's ordination reached its conclusion, I have met a number of female Church of England clergy. Such change is currently beyond the scope of Roman Catholic custom and practice and so it still takes me a few minutes to readjust my focus when a female voice invites us to pray. It is still a novelty to me but one which I quickly and happily get used to.

The reading that morning was from the *Acts of the Apostles*, the book of scripture I remember my primary school teacher encouraging me to read because, she said, "It is as exciting as any adventure story." She was right. All the ingredients are there: strong characters, great and exotic journeys, moments of high drama and miraculous escapes from danger. This is the closest we have to a reporter's account of those critical years after Jesus' death when one would expect His personal charisma to be fading amongst His followers along with His memory and His message. The fact that it did not and that the very opposite actually happened is the thing to ponder. What was it that really galvanised that broken, defeated group of supporters to carry Jesus' message with such courage and energy to so many people and places?

In this morning's reading, Peter and his friends had been called to face the religious authorities in Jerusalem who were alarmed by the apostles' rapidly growing popularity. When they met, the High Priest and his colleagues were confused by the apostles' eloquence, wondering how they could make such a well-argued case for their preaching despite being "uneducated men". They decided to act cautiously and released the apostles with no more than stern warnings to stop their preaching.[1]

The service continued and the man in the brown jacket to my left seemed to be doing fine with the prayers and responses. "That's good," I thought, "he doesn't need my help." When we came to the Sign of Peace we exchanged firm handshakes and then went up to stand side by side at Communion.

It was an intimate service, thoughtful, dignified yet informal. Rev Julia included us in the Prayers of Petition, "For Fiona and Nick as they begin their pilgrimage" and for a moment our names hung in the air before those of Augustine and Anselm, woven into the continuous spirit of this holy place.

The service ended and we stood to the side whilst Rev Julia had a few words with each member of the small congregation before they left. Finally, she was ready for us and she led us off through the body of the Cathedral towards St Anselm's chapel.

"Do you know who that was in the brown jacket beside you in the chapel?" she asked as we walked up the long side aisle. I paused and thought "Well, there was something familiar about him." Rev Julia smiled: "That was the Archbishop of Canterbury, Justin Welby. He's on holiday this week after all the busy time for him around Easter. He comes to a few services and hopes not to be recognised, so he can relax. It doesn't always work. Some visitors recognised him the other day and pursued him across the Cathedral – poor man!"

* * *

We followed Rev Julia through the quiet cathedral until we reached St Anselm's chapel. Anselm seems to have accompanied Fiona and me ever since we followed our independent paths to London from Edinburgh where we'd both been studying but had never met. In 1978, our first job at ARP involved us in morning meetings with homeless street drinkers gathered in the cassock-lined vestry of St Anselm's Anglican church at Kennington Cross near the Oval cricket ground. In recent times, our local church in Tooting Bec, south London, has Anselm as its patron saint. It is almost certain that Anselm would have visited the monastic community which once existed in the neighbourhood where we now live. The land had been handed over to the Norman Abbey of Bec after William's victory at Hastings in 1066 and, although the exact location of the monastery is uncertain, it is possible that the monks lived close to Stane Street, the old Roman road linking London Bridge with Chichester. Its route now runs along the A24 right past our church, and makes our connection with Anselm feel very real.

Whilst living at Bec in Normandy, Anselm became highly respected as a scholar and a theologian. His mentor, Lanfranc, was appointed by William the Conqueror to be the first Norman archbishop of Canterbury and on Lanfranc's death the new king, William Rufus, appointed Anselm to be his successor. In March 1093, Anselm was summoned to Gloucester where the king was gravely ill and expected to die. After making his confession, William Rufus named Anselm to be the new archbishop of Canterbury. This was the last thing that Anselm wanted. He wished to pursue a life of meditation and teaching and protested that he had neither the interest nor the aptitude for secular business. In tears, Anselm pleaded with the king to change his mind but William Rufus insisted and tried to press the pastoral staff into Anselm's clenched hand. When he failed, the bishops forced Anselm's fist open and then closed his fingers round the shaft. Then, as everyone sang and acclaimed their new archbishop, they carried Anselm into church with the crozier still jammed into his hand.[2]

Surprisingly, William Rufus recovered and lived for another seven years before being killed whilst out hunting in the New Forest. Anselm himself went on to be a skilled and effective archbishop. He succeeded in building relationships between the defeated Saxons and their new masters and it was a Saxon monk, Eadmer, who became his biographer. Anselm died on Holy Wednesday, April 21, 1109 at the age of 76 and he is still venerated in Canterbury. In a side chapel dedicated to him there is a modern altar of marble from Anselm's birthplace of Aosta. Once we had crossed the Alps, the Via Francigena would take us through this ancient Roman town.

Rev Julia invited Fiona and me to kneel here on the marble steps whilst she gave us her blessing with the words of Sr Macrina Wiederkehr's Pilgrims Prayer:

> *"May flowers spring up where your feet touch the earth. May the feet that walked before you bless your every step. May the weather that's important be the weather of your heart. May all your intentions find their way into the heart of God. May your prayers be like flowers strewn for other pilgrims. May your heart find meaning in unexpected events. May friends who are praying for you carry you along the way. May the broken world ride on your shoulders. May you carry your joy and your grief in the backpack of your soul. May you remember all the circles of prayer throughout the world."*[3]

From St Anselm's chapel, Rev Julia took us to the vestry where she stamped our pilgrims' passports and sent us on our way. We walked out of the south door, past the stone marking the official start of the Via Francigena, through the great gate of Christ Church and turned left along Burgate.

* * *

This section of the North Downs Way, leading from the main gate of Canterbury Cathedral to St Martin's hill on the edge of town, is surely one of the richest spiritual and historic routes a pilgrim can walk in England.

First, within a few hundred yards, there is the Roman Catholic church of St Thomas of Canterbury. Here, in its Martyrs' Chapel, there are (as far as I know) the only relics of Thomas Becket still in the city. A piece of bone believed to be from his finger, another sliver of bone from his body and a piece of his vestment are venerated at the chapel altar. In 1220, the Cathedral authorities had given them to a group of Cardinals from Rome who were present when the saint's body was moved to its new shrine behind the high altar. The Cardinals took the relics back home with them and so these precious fragments were safe in Europe when Becket's shrine and all that it contained were obliterated on King Henry VIII's order in 1538.

Alongside these treasures are two relics of a modern martyr canonised by Pope Francis in 2018. A display case on the wall of the Martyrs' Chapel holds two liturgical vestments, a white, full length alb and a long, thin decorated scarf (known as a stole) worn by St Oscar Romero when he was Archbishop of El Salvador from 1977 to his death on March 24, 1980. Romero was an outspoken critic of the violent regime that was then ruling the country and his growing popularity posed a serious threat to the rulers' interests. He had to be silenced. On a bright, sunny March morning Archbishop Romero was shot dead whilst saying Mass in the chapel of La Divina Providencia hospital. The murder shocked the world and galvanised international opposition against El Salvador's rulers.

These two church leaders, Becket and Romero, both realised that their challenge to state authority could cost them their lives, yet they did not hold back. Their martyrdoms inspired the people they cared for and, eventually, helped bring those in authority to account.

There is, in fact, a remarkable link between these relics of St Oscar and the circumstances of St Thomas' death. Archbishop Romero's vestments were presented to this small Canterbury church in 1997 by the Cathedral in San Salvador. In exchange, the Cathedral received a relic of St Thomas Becket that, for generations, had been held by the family of a parishioner, Eileen Evans. Eileen's maiden name was Turnham and a notice in the chapel records that one of Eileen's ancestors, Ranulf de Broc, had been involved in Thomas' murder.

De Broc had welcomed the four knights at Saltwood Castle, near Hythe, and then travelled with them to Canterbury. He commanded the troops surrounding the Cathedral whilst the four went inside to argue with Thomas and murder him. Afterwards, De Broc and the four knights searched Becket's apartments for documents to bring back to the king.

Ranulf de Broc had five daughters and one of them married Stephen of Turnham. Centuries later, Eileen Turnham and her family still felt their personal connection to the martyrdom of Thomas Becket.

Eileen's motives for her generous donation are not recorded, but there is something wonderful about this exchange of gifts. Through her, St Thomas now brings inspiration to the people of El Salvador and St Oscar Romero's modern witness is brought into Canterbury's famous story.

Sadly, on this day, there was no time to pause as the walk had to get underway. Fiona and I therefore marched quickly past not only the church of St Thomas of Canterbury, but also the ruins of St Augustine's Abbey, the site of Augustine's original grave before he was reburied in Canterbury Cathedral[4]. The way took us uphill along a main road, passing the prison on the left, before reaching the final great place of pilgrimage on this remarkable little route.

* * *

St Martin's proudly claims to be the oldest church in continuous use in the English-speaking world. Its unbroken link with the earliest days of Christianity, and its relatively remote hilltop location on the fringes of the city, make it a particularly spiritual place.

The Venerable Bede's *History*, written in AD 731, is quoted in the parish guide and tells us:

> "*On the east side of the city there was an old church in honour of St Martin, built during the Roman occupation of Britain, where the queen, who was a Christian, was accustomed to pray.*"

Queen Bertha was a Frankish princess and daughter of a king of Paris. She had been brought up near Tours where the famous St Martin had been bishop two centuries earlier. When, in the 580s she married Ethelbert, heir to the throne of Kent, one of the conditions was that she would be able to continue to worship as a Christian. Honouring his commitment, King Ethelbert gave her an old Roman building which became her royal chapel. When Augustine and his followers arrived in Canterbury in 597, Queen Bertha offered it to them to use as their base. Bede continues:

"Here they first began to assemble, to sing the psalms, to pray, to celebrate Mass, to preach and to baptise, until the king was converted to the faith and gave them greater freedom to preach and to build and restore churches everywhere."

St Martin's is not always open, but this Saturday morning we were in luck. A wedding rehearsal was in progress and we had the opportunity to step inside this wonderful little place. Signs of the original structure are still clearly visible. Long, flat red Roman bricks can be seen at the entrance to the sanctuary. Outside, they are there in abundance in the walls of the chancel. It's even possible that a bricked-up doorway could have been the entrance to Queen Bertha's original chapel. St Martin's is holy ground indeed, its Christian heritage alive and unbroken across the centuries.

Outside in the churchyard, I continued up the hill to find the grave of someone I'd never met but who, nonetheless, had been a big part of my life and deserved my thanks.

Mary Tourtel was born in Canterbury in 1874 and published her first cartoon story in the *Daily Express* on November 8, 1920. *Little Lost Bear* introduced Rupert Bear to the world, and he would go on to charm generations of children and their parents. He continues to do so to the present day.

My mum, Pamela Kempster, grew up a few miles from here in Gillingham. Mary Tourtel's Rupert stories were an important part of her childhood and she passed the books on to my sister and me so that the little bear could gain a special place in our affections too.

Tourtel's original stories include the same themes of magical adventure that are characteristic of Rupert's adventures today. However, they sometimes had a darker edge than those written by later authors. I still remember the fate of a particularly nasty character in a Tourtel story whose punishment was to be absorbed by magic into the trunk of a tree. Rupert watched as this happened and the story-teller observed that, if you looked carefully when you go walking in the woods, you could sometimes see the outline of others who had shared a similar fate. All these years later, I still look at gnarled tree trunks to see if I can spot any human features. Sometimes I think I do.

In 1935, Mary Tourtel entrusted Rupert to Alfred Bestall. When she died in 1948, she was buried with her husband on the upper slope of the graveyard surrounding St Martin's church. From here, you are almost level with the tower of the Cathedral itself. When the trees are bare in winter there is a wonderful view of the city.

Mary Tourtel's grave is simple and uncelebrated, which is a shame for someone who created so much joy in children's lives. Standing there, I remembered how the *Rupert Annual* was a regular gift in our Christmas pillowcase and how my dad clipped out the Rupert cartoon from his work colleague's *Daily Express* each day so we could assemble the full story in our own scrapbook. I remembered too, my own children, Tom and Sam, going to sleep listening to a cassette tape of their Nana and Grandad reading them Rupert stories. *Rupert and the Hazel Nut* began with my Dad's Irish voice greeting the boys:

"Hello lads. Grandad here. Are you ready for another story? Here's Nana to read you a good one this time."

Mum came in on cue: *"Right, this one's called Rupert and the Hazel Nut..."* before her normal, very professional delivery dissolved into giggles. Their laughter was like sprinkled fairy dust and I can hear it still.

* * *

We walked out of Canterbury in the company of our good friend, Chris Graham. Chris had studied social work with Fiona in Edinburgh in the 1970s and their friendship has brought me, and our sons, on countless happy visits to Kent. Her husband, Chris Morgan, has been my companion on many journeys to the Western Front but his job on this occasion was to collect our rucksacks in his car and meet us later at the end of our day's walking.

The North Downs Way led off a side road opposite the entrance to St Martin's. There was rain in the air and we recalled the prayer we'd received that morning from Rev. Julia *"May the weather that's important be the weather of your heart."* No reason to fret then! The pilgrim logo began to appear on way markers, affirming that we were now on the Via Francigena and soon we were out into open country. It was pleasant, fast walking along tarmac roads with only the occasional cyclist or dog walker to nod to as we passed. Everyone seemed to share with us the anticipation of a Saturday morning and all the promise of the weekend ahead. Soon we reached the prosperous and well cared for village of Patrixbourne. Rain clouds were gathering as we approached the Church of St Mary, one of the highlights of this section between Canterbury and Dover. Many walking guides celebrate the Norman arch and tympanum above its south entrance door. However today, in the grey light and as rain began to fall, this complex stone carving of Christ surrounded by creatures of the Apocalypse seemed weather beaten and fragile. Inside, the external wall to the east was shrouded in builders' tarpaulins and scaffolding obscured the church's famous wheel window. Overall, St Mary's felt dark and damp. It was as if we were visiting a sick, elderly relative that the builder-doctors were trying to restore to health. There was, nonetheless, a pride in the church's place on the Via Francigena and a pilgrim's passport stamp was placed on a side table, ready for our use.

The author of our guide to the North Downs Way had a dim view of the next section of the walk. Writing in 1982, Denis Herbstein observed

"There now follows some of the dreariest progress of the North Downs Way – a succession of ploughed and grazed fields on the lower side of Barham Downs."[5]

Maybe he was just having a bad day because our experience was very different. With the rain shower over, we found ourselves enjoying the wide vistas of open ground and overarching sky, the skylarks happily chattering above us and the brilliant paintbrush yellow of the oil seed rape giving dramatic colour. We paused in Womenswold to eat our sandwiches. The churchyard of St Margaret's was on a high mound from where we could look down on the occasional car weaving its way along the village's narrow street. The church itself was locked but a note displayed the address of the keyholder who was happy to open it for us. St Margaret's is a very big church for such a small village and we were told that the population had never been much bigger than its present size of just a few hundred souls. We wondered if its generous size was because of its location on the Way between Canterbury and Dover but there was nothing inside to support this theory, not even a modern pilgrim's stamp.

On the 15 kilometres from Canterbury we had not found any shops, cafes or tea stalls in the villages we passed through so the café at the East Kent Railway in Shepherdswell was a welcome place to end our day's walking. Once a busy colliery line serving the mines of Kent, the East Kent Railway's volunteers now operate 1960s diesel trains to entertain weekend visitors. We enjoyed tea and cakes surrounded by posters and photographs of the railway's glory days, displayed with all the pride and purpose that inspires railway enthusiasts across the world.

The lady serving tea told us of the time that a woman had stumbled exhausted into the café. Like us, she had walked from Canterbury on the first stage of the Via Francigena but her plan required her to be in Dover that night to catch a boat the following day. It was clear that she had badly miscalculated and now she was in a fix. She had neither the time nor the energy to complete the next 15 km. "We felt sorry for her," said our hostess, "so we offered to drive her to Dover. She was very grateful."

We would encounter many acts of generosity like this on our journey along the Via Francigena. The long-distance walker is vulnerable and such moments of kindness illuminate the spirit of the pilgrimage. I was sure that this female walker would forever celebrate Shepherdswell railway station as a place where she had been blessed by the kindness of strangers.

We spent the night at Chris and Chris' home by the coast at Kingsdown then resumed our walk next day from Shepherdswell. The path took us through the estate of Waldershare House, home to the Earl of Guilford. The mansion itself was tucked away at the foot of two hills, as if sheltering from the weather and the world. An inscription engraved over old stable gates exhorted us in Latin to *"Disce Vivere"* or *"Learn to Live"* a phrase which seemed to beg more questions than it gave answers. The Church of All Saints stood in a grove of trees beyond but our visit did not yield a pilgrim stamp, nor any memorable insights. Far more exciting was the appearance soon afterwards of a new red and white waymark which proclaimed that we were also on the Jerusalem Way.

All the great routes to the landmarks of Christendom seemed to be converging as we joined the well-defined, arrow straight route of the ancient Roman road connecting the Roman port of Richborough, near Sandwich, and Dover itself. Frequently, the path ran along deep cuttings. With hedgerows high and tree tops linking overhead, it seemed the sun might never reach the ground on which we walked. Indeed, one 100 metre section was such a quagmire that we had to hang on to branches and thorn bushes to walk along the slippery side of the bank. It was a reminder of what the early pilgrims faced and why, for centuries, rivers were such a popular means of transport.

Crossing the A2 dual carriageway, we began our descent into Dover. A rusting barbed wire fence ran beside the path and along the edge of a field. It was constructed using standard issue British army screw pickets – iron poles nearly six feet in length, twisted at the top and middle to create loopholes through which the lines of barbed wire are threaded. The Military School and barracks were nearby and the castle sat proudly on its hilltop above the harbour. This was fortress Dover, England's front-line town since Roman times and the gateway to Europe. The barbed wire fence with its leaning picket poles anticipated the next stage of the walk. This would follow the last defences of the British army's 1940 retreat to Dunkirk and the line of the Western Front in 1914–18. Such picket poles were key to protecting the trench lines and they still litter the battlefields to this day.

* * *

Dover town had a quiet, sombre Sunday afternoon feel to it as the rain began to fall again. The parish church in the high street was open, but the warden I spoke to had not heard of the Via Francigena nor knew anything about a pilgrim stamp. Dover's real pilgrim shrine was tucked behind the high street shops a short walk away, but it was closed and its secrets ignored as traffic whizzed by.

The Chapel of St Edmund was rediscovered in August 1943 when two shops on Priory Road were destroyed by artillery shells fired from France. As the debris was cleared away, a remarkable chapel was revealed. Consecrated by St Richard of Chichester to the memory of his old friend, St Edmund of Abingdon, it was here on March 30, 1253 that Richard said his last Mass before collapsing and dying four days later. The first words of his famous prayer were recorded on his deathbed:

"Thanks be to Thee my Lord Jesus Christ, for all the benefits which Thou hast given me, for all the pains and insults which Thou hast borne for me."

Before taking his body to be buried in Chichester Cathedral, 100 miles away, Richard's followers removed the heart and internal organs (the *viscera*) and placed them in a small chalk-lined pit under the Chapel's altar. When Richard was canonised in 1262, St Edmund's Chapel became a popular place of pilgrimage for those in search of healing from the saint.

With the Dissolution of the Monasteries, St Edmund's Chapel was lost and forgotten and by 1943 it was being used as a workshop. Despite its lucky escape from shellfire, post war redevelopment once more threatened its existence. In the 1960s, a local Roman Catholic priest, Fr Terence Tanner, led a campaign to save it from demolition and raised funds for its restoration. In 1968 the Chapel was reconsecrated and the Abbey of Pontigny, where St Edmund's shrine still stands, donated a small relic of the saint to place in a niche in the south wall.

Remarkably, three quarters of the original chapel building still survives and archaeologists have even discovered the cist under the altar which once contained St Richard's remains. Above it, a three-inch diameter angled hole can still be seen in the stone floor. This would have held a piece of wood, known as a "touching stick", which enabled medieval pilgrims to indirectly touch the buried holy relic whilst praying for the benefits of its healing powers.

The Chapel is now in the care of the ecumenical St Edmund Memorial Trust and has claimed the honour of being the smallest church in regular use in England. These days, the Chapel's heavy oak door is usually locked but, as we finished this English stage of our walk, I remembered one Saturday morning Mass I had attended there many years before with my young son, Tom. It was a grey, foggy December morning and about 20 people had filled the simple stone building. With only two stone benches to sit on, everyone had decided to stand in a half circle against the walls and close to the altar. It was a very intimate gathering.

Fr Ryan of St Paul's parish in Dover welcomed us and explained that Mass would be said in Latin. When he learnt that I was a visitor, Fr Ryan invited me to read the Epistle (in English). I felt honoured. The chapel was very dark and the only light came from the candles burning on the altar. The lectionary rested on a cushion on the right side of the altar and when I stepped forward to read I had to peer through the gloom to make out the words. In the candlelight, all was just as it would have been those many centuries before.

The Saturday morning Masses are less frequent now, perhaps because there are fewer priests available. If Dover is ever to take its pilgrim credentials seriously there would be no better place to receive its stamp than here at St Edmund's Chapel.

* * *

1. *Acts of the Apostles*, Chapter 4, verses 1 to 22.

2. See *St Anselm: A Portrait in a Landscape* by R.W. Southern, Cambridge University Press 1990, for a full account of the unusual circumstances of Anselm's appointment as Archbishop.

3. Sr Macrina Wiederkehr OSB was a member of the community at St Scholastica Monastery in Fort Smith, Arkansas, USA. She died in 2020. https://stscho.org/macrina.php

4. We did not know it at the time, but, a few miles along the coast, at Ramsgate, close to where Augustine and his companions came ashore in AD 597, a new Shrine to St Augustine was about to be inaugurated in the famous church designed by Augustus Pugin. In celebration, the Fathers of the Oxford Oratory had donated a small piece of bone – a relic of St Augustine himself which had been kept in Europe and had therefore survived the destruction of the Reformation.

5. Herbstein, *The North Downs Way* page 127.

"If Dover is ever to take its pilgrim credentials seriously there would be no better place to receive its stamp than here at St Edmund's Chapel."

CHAPTER THREE

Towards the Front

Dover, Calais and Dunkirk

The sun woke me at 5 am and Chris' son-in-law, Sean, kindly drove me the few miles from Kingsdown to the ferry port at Dover. The sky was clear and by 7 am the day already felt hot. Sean dropped me at the Arrivals zone and I shouldered my pack for the first time. Although much lighter than Fr Gerry Hughes' 34-pound load (which included a tent) I was rather anxious about how I would manage the 17-pound weight over the days to come. For now, it sat comfortably on my back, and I felt up for the adventure. I'd booked onto the 9.30 am sailing but, to my delight, the check-in staff were happy for me to join the 8 am crossing. It was as if I'd been given an extra hour's holiday. I found a seat in the open air at the stern of *The Pride of Kent* and looked back at the famous cliffs of Dover.

I knew the scene well. To the right of the cutting where the A2 dual carriageway slices its way through the chalk cliffs I could make out the cluster of low trees and shrubs where, in the 1990s, a homeless Russian used to camp. I'd met him once when Tom and I were walking the clifftop path. A wild looking bearded figure wearing a long, grimy overcoat had called to us from his shelter of plastic sheeting stretched between the tree branches. A fire burnt below a blackened pot and a line of string ran across the clearing at head-height. From the line there hung little plastic bags containing soft, moist parcels of an unknown and ominous substance. We ventured no further.

The conversation started normally enough as he told us how as a teenager in Russia he had escaped the Stalinists only to be captured and put to work by the Nazis. Somehow, he survived and after the war he'd made his way through Europe and across the Channel. It was a remarkable story and I was in awe of what he had endured. However, the more he spoke, the more his paranoia and his anger became evident. Soon he was ranting. There were conspiracies at every level of society, Communist, Fascist, trust no one. We made our excuses and walked on leaving him calling his warnings to us long after we were out of sight. Further down the path, we met another walker who told us that the Russian was a well-known local character. Sadly, he was sometimes taunted by youths who had no sense of wonder at what such a man had seen and survived in his long and troubled life.

As *The Pride of Kent* pulled out into the Channel I noticed a smear of yellow in the atmosphere along the top of the cliffs. With the sun out to sea behind me the colour contrasted starkly with the clear blue of the sky above it. Here was tangible evidence of the pollution created by the Monday morning rush hour. I was glad to be out of it but troubled that despite all our progress in cleaning up our environment there is still so much to do.

* * *

There were only ten foot passengers gathered beside our exit door as the ferry docked at Calais. Foot passengers are rare these days and I felt part of an exclusive group. A bus took us to the terminal from where I followed signs to the town centre over a kilometre away. The walkway was encased in steel and wire and after a hundred yards or so I suddenly realised that there was no sign of the other foot passengers. Cars and lorries drove away in the distance and for the first time on this expedition I felt isolated in a vast concrete landscape in a very different country. I was glad to reach the port's boundary and see a familiar Via Francigena pilgrim sign pinned to the fence. It was a comforting reminder that this was all part of a plan connecting me to Canterbury and to Rome.

Approaching the edge of the town I came to what remained of the old port area. Rusting railway tracks ran from derelict warehouses onto the open waterside expanses of cracked concrete and scrub. I could see makeshift tents on the wasteland and people moving slowly around. As I got closer I realised that these were not the usual homeless people I routinely saw in London. From their appearance I guessed most had come from Africa. They were now camped here waiting for a chance to make a final crossing into the UK.

In later years, the world's spotlight would focus on their plight and the dilemmas posed by "The Jungle" encampment as it grew ever bigger on the edge of Calais. However, in 2014 there was little media attention and I was shocked to discover how many people were living in such primitive conditions. I estimated there were about 100 permanent shelters of wood and plastic sheeting with clothes and sleeping bags hung out to dry on the wire fence enclosing the land. Young men (they were all young men) in their 20s and 30s wandered back and forth or stood in groups chatting, their features darkened and weather-beaten by long hours spent outdoors. The sun was strong but, despite the heat, they were all wearing layers of clothing with jackets or anoraks buttoned over sweaters. These men had nowhere safe to leave their belongings and had to wear everything they had.

It reminded me of the scene in "The Bullring" encampment at London's Waterloo Bridge in the 1990s but there was one big difference. The men who had slept in the shanty town shelters that filled the underpasses around Waterloo station were, by and large, middle-aged and broken in spirit. However, these men encamped at Calais seemed youthful and full of energy. It had taken a lot of courage and enterprise to get this far and I was sorry to see such talent wasting away.

There was no sign that any police or others in authority were supervising this space and I became conscious that I was a lone walker with a small camera at my belt and Euros in my pocket. I would have liked to stop and learn something of the circumstances that had brought these young men here but I did not expect to speak their language and I was anxious about how obvious and isolated I was. Embarrassed, too, at the indulgence of my own unnecessary walk. Neither terror, nor poverty were driving me onward. Our lives felt very far apart and so, partly out of self-preservation, partly out of shame, I chose to keep on walking and avoid catching anyone's eye.

* * *

As the ferry had approached the port, I had noticed the huge, dark grey shapes of collapsed gun emplacements along the beach. They sat like elephant turds on the yellow sand, lingering defecations from the Second World War. In Calais itself, I discovered another grey concrete edifice sitting like a giant slug amidst the delicate gardens of the pretty Parc de St Pierre. This wartime communications centre now housed a museum recalling the Nazi occupation. As I studied the exhibits, my Anglocentric perspective was shaken by the details of daily life under a tyrannical regime. The town had been captured on May 26, 1940 and a poster issued soon after by the new authorities instructed French and Belgian refugees on the routes they should take leaving the town. They were not allowed to use public transport so they had to cycle, or walk to their destinations. Another poster, in English, was addressed to "All English People Living in Calais" and instructed them to report to the authorities immediately. If they did not, they would be assumed to be spies and "treated accordingly".

My parents and grandparents spoke of "The War" in a matter of fact way and usually in reference to time. Events were either "Before the War", "During the War" or "After the War". Throughout my life I had been aware of the war as something that had happened in another time and another place. The Battle of Britain had kept invasion from our shores so that "The War" remained in that faraway place called Europe, in a time long long ago.

Now, in this cold, stark bunker I read the original notices and posters of instructions and penalties for disobedience, the mundane bureaucratic tools of fear and persecution, and realised that "The War" was no longer "over there", it was here in all the day to day fear and persecution of Nazi occupation. Such details brought home to me just how important it had been for Britain and her Allies to win the conflict.

Sometimes when speaking with my grandmother I had to check whether it was the First or the Second World War she was referring to as "The War", but historians make the connection between the two great conflicts very clear. Indeed, the more I have read the more it has seemed to me that the beginning of the Second World War was really the continuation, after a long armistice, of events that had only been paused in 1918. For a lad like me born in the 1950s, this huge event had happened just beyond the horizon of my consciousness and I had taken the peace and prosperity that Britain enjoyed afterwards for granted. Now, on the centenary of the start of that first conflict it seemed only right that my route to Rome should take a detour to follow the line which from 1914 to 1918 marked the edge of unoccupied Europe.

The German invasion of 1914 had as its primary aim the speedy capture of the Channel ports of France and Belgium. This was never achieved. However, in 1940 the German army's rapid advance could not be stopped and the story of 1914 was rewritten as France collapsed and soldiers of Britain's small Expeditionary Force, many still equipped with the same arms and equipment of 1918, were rolled back to the sea.

It could be said that Dunkirk is the place where the First World War finally ended. It was where Britain's army, which had held the line so defiantly from 1914, was at last driven out of France and it was where I'd decided that my walk through France and Belgium should properly begin.

* * *

The ferries to Dunkirk do not accept foot passengers. You must travel by car or with a bicycle to be allowed on board. So, with my plans to sail direct to Dunkirk thwarted, I had decided that it was legitimate to take a bus from Calais to travel the 30 kilometres to get there. By mid-afternoon

I had checked into the small Hotel Dunkerque Centre Gare and was ready to explore.

The German army launched its assault on France in the early hours of May 10, 1940. To everyone's astonishment less than three weeks later, on May 29, the British public were informed that the British Expeditionary Force (BEF) was being evacuated from the beaches and harbour of Dunkirk. The call went out for civilian vessels to assist the ships of the Royal Navy and many crews responded. It was a desperate move with little hope of success. However, the story of "the Little Ships" of Operation Dynamo became the stuff of legend and transformed one of the greatest defeats that Britain had ever experienced into an inspiring and heroic miracle.

For reasons that are still debated, Hitler held his panzer tanks back from delivering a killer blow to the beleaguered forces gathered in the town and in the sand dunes nearby. Instead, the Luftwaffe constantly bombed the ships and the soldiers queuing to escape, whilst the main thrust of the German effort was directed elsewhere. When Operation Dynamo began, its ambition to rescue up to 45,000 troops seemed wildly optimistic.[1] By the time that German forces entered the town on June 4 the evacuation had succeeded in bringing back to England some 338,000 men, about 229,000 of whom were British with the others being French and Belgian.[2] This was far more than the 11,000 British soldiers killed and the 41,000 captured or missing during the campaign. [3] It was a remarkable outcome.

The army lost huge quantities of weapons and equipment in France and many soldiers would wait for years before they were sufficiently re-equipped to be able to fight a battle again. However, this was far less important than the fact that so many men were saved to fight another day. The country's fragile confidence was boosted by an heroic story that spoke directly to the identity of this small island nation, Great Britain.

Dunkirk itself was devastated and few buildings of that time escaped damage or destruction. The waterfront area I walked through now was a succession of modern glass and metal shops and restaurants but I found one veteran of the evacuation at anchor in the harbour. The paddle steamer *Princess Elizabeth* bore witness to those epic events of 1940 just as the magnificent imposing belfry of the Hotel de Ville reminded visitors of the grandeur of the town's pre-war past. However, it was the little chapel of Our Lady of the Dunes which provided me with the lasting memory of my visit.

The chapel was the only place of Catholic worship I could find open that Monday evening. Damaged in 1940, it has a long history of surviving the many wars and battles that have swept through this town. A parish leaflet by André Merck explained that when the chapel was founded in 1403 the port was in Flemish territory. War had ravaged the district and the Duke of Burgundy decided to strengthen the town's waterfront fortifications. During their construction, workmen discovered a freshwater spring that was uncontaminated by the nearby sea water. This was good news. Freshwater supplies were vital to any community, particularly one which might be besieged. However, to add blessings to this discovery, the workmen also uncovered from the sand a small statue of Our Lady holding the infant Jesus. She may have been washed ashore from the wreck of a ship but no one really knew and many were soon wondering if her appearance was in fact a miracle.

Attempts to move the statue were foiled. The story goes that whenever the figure was taken to another place it used to disappear only to be found again close to the spring. It seemed that the Virgin's will was clear and so a little chapel was built on the site to accommodate her.

In the centuries that followed, the tiny chapel escaped several raids including the French army's destruction of Dunkirk in 1558. However, when new fortifications were built in the 17th century by that master of defensive construction, Vauban, it became isolated from the town. The Treaty of Utrecht between France, Britain and Spain in 1713 reopened access to the chapel but the French Revolution in 1789 threatened it once more. Scornful of its "superstitious" heritage, the authorities used it as a cartridge factory until it was completely destroyed when the gunpowder stocks exploded in 1794.

Happily, "superstitions" were rooted in deep faith and affection. When the revolutionaries seized the chapel building parishioners took the statue of the Virgin and Child into hiding and kept it safe until the chapel could be rebuilt in 1816. However, the threats to its safety continued, first in 1870 when the Franco-Prussian war humbled the French nation and again in 1914 when war returned once more. The custodians pledged that, should Dunkirk escape destruction, they would extend this sacred place in thanksgiving. The promise had to wait to be honoured until after the end of the Second World War but kept it was and now I was standing in a little garden outside an attractive and substantial brick-built church on the busy Rue de Leughenaer.

* * *

Sr Jeanne-Marie arrived with the key to open the door. She apologised that it was locked but they just didn't have enough people to watch over it all the time. Inside, when she turned on the lights I discovered a charming little space with a blue painted ceiling dotted with numerous white stars. It was just as the heavens might appear to sailors navigating their way at sea and, sure enough, hanging from the roof was a fleet of beautifully crafted models of sailing ships and boats. This was the spiritual home of a seafaring community.

That evening, I was one of eight people, six women and two men, who had gathered for Vespers. Even with this small number, the church felt homely and we divided up either side of the aisle to respond to the chants and prayers that Sr Jeanne-Marie would be leading.

Before we'd begun, Sr Jeanne-Marie had spoken to me rapidly in French and I had nodded, dumbly. It was only later that I realised that she'd given me a job to do. As the service neared its end, two ladies behind me each read a prayer of intercession. I looked at the prayer sheet. There were more. Should I go next? I froze, not wanting to do the wrong thing and, after a moment, the lady in front of me said the next one. There was one prayer left and there was another woman ahead who had not yet said anything.

I hoped I'd escaped, but she said nothing. I waited and the pause became longer. Behind me, the two ladies exchanged whispered comments and a faint "tut-tutting". The lady in front of me turned and gestured to me to get on with it. So, with a loud voice and my best schoolboy French I read the final prayer.

The prayers ended and Sr Jeanne-Marie brought the Blessed Sacrament from its tabernacle. She placed the small, round white wafer in the window of the monstrance, an ornate vessel which takes its name from the Latin word *monstrare*, "to show". Sr Jeanne-Marie then carried the Blessed Sacrament to the altar where it could be seen and we all knelt in silence.

To the outsider, this can seem a very strange thing. The exhibition of a wafer of bread in an extravagantly decorated ornament which the people then kneel before in great reverence. Might this be idolatry?

The Roman Catholic belief is that during the Mass, at the moment of consecration, the wafer of bread and the cup of wine become the Body and Blood of Jesus himself. This is not merely symbolic, it is a change in the very substance of these everyday things. Just as when ice becomes water and water becomes steam the essential H_2O formula of atoms is still the same, so the belief teaches that the bread and wine, whilst still being bread and wine, become the Real Presence of Jesus in our material lives.

Stories of blood dripping from a consecrated host are celebrated as tangible proof of the truth of this belief.[4] Some of these accounts are very recent, but I'm not so sure. I feel on safer ground in trying to understand the belief in Jesus' Real Presence when I consider my wedding ring. This ring has been created from gold, a very tangible metal. Its presence on my finger is a symbol, a visual sign of my married status. However, if I were to lose the ring it would be hard just to shrug my shoulders and buy another one. Inside the ring, Fiona's name and mine are inscribed together with the date of our marriage. In truth, our marriage has transformed that band of metal and imbued it with a lifetime's love. It is no longer what it was when it was first made. Yes, it is still gold and yes, it is a common symbol of marriage but it is also so much more. Material things do change, but to appreciate that change we must first be open to the possibility that it can happen.

So, as we sat and knelt in silence, this exposition of the Blessed Sacrament emphasised the sacred nature of this chapel whilst our restless minds were challenged to settle and be at peace in the presence of a power far greater than ourselves.

It was a very peaceful 40 minutes. At the end, after the Sacrament had been returned to its tabernacle and those gathered began to say their farewells to each other, I waited my turn to speak to Sr Jeanne-Marie. I wanted to find out more about the statue of Our Lady and the Child Jesus that was at the heart of this chapel's story. My turn came. *"Je suis Anglais,"* I began. Did her eyes roll slightly upwards, I wondered, as she replied *"Je connais! – I know!"*? Clearly my schoolboy French was not as good as I thought it was and I wondered what howlers I might have committed in my clumsy mispronunciations of the final prayer.

Sr Jeanne-Marie was, however, kind and patient. I managed to convey my interest in the statue of Our Lady. "Is it still here?" I asked. "Oh yes," she said and pointed to a shrine above the altar. There, on a plinth of white lace was a small figurine about two foot tall. It was the image of a woman dressed in robes of blue-grey and red, wearing a crown and carrying a child. Surrounded by heavy clouds of white stucco, it was as if she was looking down on us from a chalk cave. I was so pleased that Our Lady of the Dunes had survived after all that she had endured.

* * *

Dunkirk is where several canals that run through France and Belgium reach the sea. The British used these in 1940 to establish a defensive perimeter around the town stretching from Nieuport and Furnes to the east through to Bergues to the south and along the north–south line of the Canal de Mardyck to the west. In this way, Dunkirk was enclosed in an uneven salient of waterways jutting out from the coast that was, at most, around 7 miles (11km) deep and about 25 miles (40km) wide. French and British soldiers were thinly spread along this frontier, concentrating their guard on the few bridges across the canals that had been kept open for retreating soldiers. The risk, of course, was that German tanks could follow them.

My plan was to follow the innermost canal, the Canal de Dunkerque à Furnes that ran parallel to the coast and about a mile inland. After about 13 miles (21km), at Furnes, I would pick up another canal to take me to my next night's accommodation in the Belgian town of Nieuport. That way, I reasoned, I would be sure of my route and remain engaged with the history of the defensive struggle to protect the evacuation.

However, I was also aware that it was a long way on the map to I Nieuport. I estimated that the distance was about 20 miles (32km) and I was conscious that this would be my first full day's walking with my pack. Another hot day like the one I'd spent in Calais could knock me out, so I decided to get on the road as early as I could.

A mix of excitement and anxiety woke me long before my alarm clock rang. At 3.30 am I was fully packed and standing outside the hotel, ready to be on my way. A half-moon shone brightly in the southern sky and at an intersection of waterways, I paused to study my map and find the correct canal to follow. There was magic in the dark, silent town at this hour of the morning. The cars and the people were all asleep but the canal locks with their huge sluice gates, bridges and docks were like living creatures of wood and iron, pulsing with the energy of the weight and volume of the water they held in check.

Finding the right route was trickier than I'd imagined. Several stretches of water converged then divided and it was not until I saw a Commonwealth War Graves sign pointing into a dark wooded area to my right that I was reassured that I had found the correct path. I set off confidently along the left bank of the canal past rows of redbrick terraced cottages until open fields gave me a view looking back and across to the spot lit belfries of Saint-Eloi and the Hotel de Ville in the distance. I was making great progress and when I saw a road sign saying "Furnes 20km" I thought "I'll be there by 9 am."

Then the way stopped. A water channel came in from my left, cutting across the path and joining the canal itself on my right. There were no bridges so I was forced to turn left and follow the side of the channel into a large area of earthworks. Freshly excavated mountains of soil towered on either side above me as I followed a dirt road and wondered if I might be going further into the middle of a landfill site.

Getting lost is a feature of any walk through unknown territory. When it happens, the question is whether to turn back to a point where the way was certain or to press on and trust that things will work out. My watch told me it was 5 am and it was now fully light. I could see a gate at the end of the track, but would I be able to get through? I took a chance and pressed on.

The gate was locked and the signs on the other side forbade anyone from coming through onto the land where I now stood. Fortunately, despite the height and solidness of the gate, there were two gaps between it and the fence on either side. Even with my pack, I had no difficulty slipping through and I was thankful for the shoddy workmanship that had enabled my escape.

I was now in an industrial area where parked articulated lorries slumbered with their engines running. Signs pointed to an Ascometal factory where even at this early hour I could hear the sound of tumbling piles of metal. Somewhere in the distance, a forklift truck was ferrying scrap from one container and pouring it into another. The village of Valdunes hadn't woken up yet and as I walked through its silent streets I noticed a small memorial dedicated "*Aux victims de l'amiante de l'usine des dunes*". It was a different kind of war memorial: "To the victims of the asbestos from the factory of the dunes".

The road drew me closer to the sea and to the great strip of sand dunes that run beside the beach. Here, in May 1940, the assembling troops had gathered in their thousands to queue and wait and pray for a place on a ship to take them to England. Gunner Lieutenant Elliman, with 40 men from his unit, had driven over 20 miles from his base at Poperinge in Belgium to find safety at the coast. In World War One, Poperinge had been famous for the rest and recreation it offered British troops. Then, it had been at a safe distance from the guns pounding the town of Ypres, which was key to Britain's defence of the Channel ports. However, in 1940 there was no solid line to protect Ypres and Poperinge from the Germans' rapid advance and so Elliman and his men had been instructed to head for Dunkirk. Once they reached the port's perimeter, Military Police told them to leave their truck in a field full of other abandoned and burning vehicles and make the rest of their way on foot.

When they got into Dunkirk, in the early afternoon of May 29, 1940, a desperate scene greeted them.

"The tide was fairly low. A steamer lay on her side at the water's edge. The sandy beach was about 100 yards wide. Down the centre stood the line of men, three abreast. The smoke... from the burning oil tanks drifted eastwards over the town. A few officers walked up and down. All was quiet. And then it started! A formation of high fliers came up from the west, and dropped stick after stick of bombs... This first attack was most unnerving. You felt so completely exposed on the beach... For a time, some of us huddled under the hull of the wrecked steamer, but as nothing happened for some time, I called in all my men, and formed them up in the queue again for fear we should lose our place."

The attacks continued through the afternoon. Most were aimed at the ships gathered offshore, but, in the early evening, a Stuka dive bomber switched its focus to the waiting soldiers.

"I heard the Stuka coming down in a vertical dive right on top of me," Elliman reported. *"I was by now dulled by hours... of explosions... so that the imminence of death aroused no great feeling of fear... Either the bomb would land on me, or it wouldn't... I thought... of Margaret*

in those few seconds of suspense, and she brought me a certain peace of spirit. The next moment: Crash! Darkness! And then a vision of falling sand in front of me... I realised I had been missed, and... I could hear the plane climbing away over Dunkirk. The attack was now over."

Elliman was unhurt, but two of his men were killed, and his medical orderly's cheek had been blown away. One soldier was so shocked by the injuries he saw that he became hysterical and was carried away laughing uncontrollably.

Elliman's hopes of getting away that night were dashed.

"Thousands of men stretched away behind us, but we failed to move forward. Only the wounded were got away that night... As the hours went by, the spirits of all must have been sinking... Mine certainly were. Sleep was impossible. It was just waiting, waiting, waiting."[5]

My road curved round the edge of the Ascometal factory. I saw a path off to my left leading into the dunes and decided to follow it. Now I could hear birdsong that was louder than the "crunch" of moving metal from the factory behind me. The air smelt fresh, the vegetation nourished by overnight dew and, as I passed between trees and bushes, invisible strands of half made spiders' webs broke across my face. I walked on sand but this wasn't just a few hillocks of beach covered in scrub. The Dunes were broad and deep and high, in some places as tall as two-storey houses. This was a secret world of such scale that an army of thousands could, indeed, shelter here away from the dive-bombing and machine-gun fire.

At a crossroads of paths, I noticed some rusting railway tracks on concrete sleepers running into bushes. I looked again at the only map I had that was copied from Hugh Sebag-Montefiore's account of the battle for Dunkirk.[6] Along with the lines of the outer and inner defensive perimeters and the canals and the main roads of 1940, a railway line was indeed shown threading its way east through the Dunes from Dunkirk to Furnes and beyond. This was what I had found.

I followed its course through cuttings driven deep through the high ground and along lines of track half exposed in tangles of grass and scrub. I stopped beside a trackside maintenance box and flipped open the unlocked lid. Inside, the fuses looked as new as the day they'd been installed. It was as if, on a given moment, the world had just walked away from this railway line and did not come back.

The track led me to an abandoned station, its cracked and broken sign declaring that this was "...*RIUM MARITIME DE ZUYDCO...TE*". Here was an important place in the Dunkirk story. Built in 1910, the sanatorium at Zuydcoote was a state-of-the-art hospital where 1,400 patients could be treated in fresh air beside the sea. During the evacuation of 1940, those too ill to be taken to the ships were looked after here by volunteers from the Royal Army Medical Corps until German forces arrived to take the wounded and their carers into captivity.

I left the Dunes close to where the modern Maritime Hospital carries on its healing work and followed side roads down to the beach itself. It was not yet 7 am and the sky still had that gentle early morning promise of a new day. I trudged along the sand and paused at a graffiti-covered wartime bunker that was slowly being absorbed by the shifting beach. The view back to Dunkirk was stunning. Grey smoke from the port's industrial complex coiled into the clear blue sky. It was as if the area was still smouldering from the battles of 1940.

* * *

The imposing church of Our Lady of Bray Dunes was open. Its candles were lit and its bells chimed the eighth hour but no one was at their prayers. I paused beside the framed photograph of an elderly monk whose lined face held an open, friendly expression above his grey straggly beard. This was Blessed Frédéric Janssoone, a local Franciscan who had gained an international reputation for his work in the Holy Land and Canada during the 19th century. Pope John Paul II had acknowledged the strength of his case for sainthood by beatifying him in 1988. Blessed Frédéric 's birthplace, Ghyvelde, was a mile or two inland and I headed towards it to re-join the canal I'd been following. At the bridge over the waterway I spotted a café and decided to stop for breakfast. It was 9 am, I was nowhere near Furnes and I was ready to feast on omelette and fresh bread at Café Pont de Ghyvelde.

The Inner Perimeter to which French and British troops withdrew during the final days of the defence of Dunkirk ran just to the east of where I sat, cutting the canal at right angles before swinging south-west past the village of Ghyvelde itself. However, there was to be no "last ditch" stand along the line. As the final ship cast off from the port of Dunkirk at 3.40 am on the morning of June 4, 1940, soldiers filtered back to the beaches and prepared for captivity. Staff Officer Hauptmann Drescher entered Dunkirk with the German forces later that day and wrote:

> *"It's a complete mess. There are guns everywhere, as well as countless vehicles, corpses, wounded men and dead horses. The heat makes the whole place stink. Dunkirk itself has been completely destroyed. There are lots of fires burning... we cannot swim since the water is full of oil from the sunk ships, and is also full of corpses..."*[7]

With Paris occupied, the French announced their surrender on June 17, and, five days later, on June 22, an armistice was signed. To emphasise that this was, indeed, unfinished business Hitler decreed that the surrender document should be signed in the Compiègne Forest at the exact same place where Germany had been humiliated in 1918. The Armistice to end the Great War had been signed here in a railway carriage and this was taken out from the site's museum and moved several metres to the very spot where it had stood on November 11, 1918. Hitler had served as a corporal in the First War and now as Germany's Führer he sat in the same chair from which Marshall Foch, France's Supreme Commander, had dictated terms in 1918. However, Hitler only attended the start of proceedings on June 21. Just as Foch had done, Hitler left the carriage in a calculated gesture of disdain towards his conquered enemies and left his generals to conclude matters. Three days later, the Armistice site was demolished on Hitler's orders and the railway carriage taken to Germany to be put on display as a war trophy. In the summer of 1940, with France conquered and Britain fragile and alone, it seemed that Germany's First World War ambitions had finally been achieved.

* * *

1. *Dunkirk – Fight to the Last Man* by Hugh Sebag-Montefiore, Penguin 2007, paperback page 254. Copyright © Hugh Sebag-Montefiore 2015. Reprinted by permission of Penguin Books Limited.
2. *All Hell Broke Loose – the World at War 1939-1945*, by Max Hastings, Harper Press 2011, hardback edition, page 67
3. *Op. cit.* Hugh Sebag-Montefiore, paperback page 506. I have rounded the figures to the nearest thousand.
4. One of the most famous is an incident in 1263 in Bolsena, on the route of the Via Francigena, just 129 km from Rome. As he said the words of the Consecration, a doubting priest saw blood dripping from the host he was holding. His faith was restored, and a miracle proclaimed. Raphael depicted the scene in a famous fresco for the Vatican. The blood-stained cloth which caught the drops as they fell onto the altar is kept in the Italian Cathedral at Orvieto where it is still deeply revered. An internet search of "Eucharistic Miracles" reveals other more recent examples, including one in Buenos Aires in 1996 when Archbishop Jorge Bergoglio (who later became Pope Francis) commissioned scientific tests on a consecrated host that appeared to have become human flesh and blood.
5. *Op. cit.* Hugh Sebag-Montefiore, chapter 29, pages 384 to 387
6. *Ibid.* Hugh Sebag-Montefiore, Map 16 pages 532, 533
7. *Ibid.* Hugh Sebag-Montefiore, chapter 34, pages 456, 457

"The view back to Dunkirk was stunning. Grey smoke from the port's industrial complex coiled into the clear blue sky. It was as if the area was still smouldering from the battles of 1940."

CHAPTER FOUR

Belgium

Veurne to Nieuport

The road to Belgium was long, straight and functional. A petrol station with the word TABAC painted white on its sloping roof marked the border with France. A little further on, the shops in Adenkirke still promoted the old "duty free" culture of alcohol and tobacco but it seemed to me that the town was struggling. The exception was Titi's Palace. Here on a street corner a tribe of garden gnomes with long white beards and red hats spilled out onto the pavement. Watching over them through plate glass windows a footballer, a giraffe and an elephant shared the shelves with Our Lady, Padre Pio and Jesus himself. Bright colours and tacky taste in joyful abundance.

I left the canal and followed a country lane winding towards Furnes, now signposted in Flemish as Veurne. As the spires of the town appeared on the skyline, a peloton of 20 teenage cyclists approached. The two leaders veered towards me left hands outstretched muttering gruff words in teenage Belgian. They passed before I realised what was expected but others following did the same. I raised my left hand and our "high fives" connected at a rapid closing speed. Such respect lifted me in my tiredness and inspired me to renew my efforts.

I liked Veurne as soon as I entered it. Walking through its medieval streets, I was welcomed by a stone tableau of Christ with his 12 apostles set high in the wall of a house. A few yards further on I slumped into a chair outside the pleasant 'T Hof van de Hemel tearoom and ordered soup and a pot of Earl Grey tea. It was 12 noon and, with detours, I'd done many more than the 20kms I'd seen advertised on the road sign leaving Dunkirk. I was exhausted and very thirsty and I wondered if I had enough strength to finish the last 10kms into Nieuport. Happily, lunch and the prospect of discovering a new historic town revived my spirits. Around Veurne's central square there were splendid ancient buildings built from the wealth of centuries of successful agriculture and trade. I headed straight towards one of them, the great gothic Church of Saint Walburga.

Walburga was in fact born in England, in Devon, the daughter of a West Saxon under-king who was also the brother in law of the famous St Boniface. Walburga's father was determined to visit the Holy Land so, in AD 720, he had set out with his two sons, Willibald and Winibald, along the Via Francigena. Sadly, his pilgrimage came to a premature end when he died of a fever in Tuscany. He was buried in Lucca and his tomb became a focus for miracles and pilgrimage. Walburga's father's original name is unknown but the people of Lucca remember him to this day as St Richard the Pilgrim.

Walburga was too young for the journey and stayed behind to be educated by the nuns of Wimborne Abbey in Dorset. In adulthood, she and her two brothers joined Boniface in his mission to evangelise the pagan Germans and the trio became very well known. Veneration followed their deaths and all were eventually canonised.

Statues and reliquaries of all three stood in an aisle at the back of the church in Veurne but there were no worshippers. The shrine did not draw you to prayer, but to history. A photograph in a display case pointed tantalisingly towards the Church's most sacred relic, a fragment of the True Cross. Alas, I could not locate it in my hurried search of the various chapels. I was conscious of time and the distance I still had to travel to Nieuport. I hoped to meet St Richard the Pilgrim again when my own journey along the Via Francigena reached Lucca.

* * *

In May 1940, the canal between Veurne and Nieuport formed the final section of the defensive perimeter around Dunkirk. It is a pretty, tree-lined stretch of water that is barely the width of a Victorian municipal swimming bath. It didn't seem much of a defence, even a poor swimmer like me could cross it easily. The German troops did try using rubber boats or hiding between horses and cattle to cross one of the few remaining bridges. At Wulpen, a group had even tried to get across dressed as nuns, but the defenders managed to foil all these small incursions.

This afternoon, the canal path was busy with cyclists. Hovering over a field to my left, a military helicopter manoeuvred a heavy load hanging below it on a cable. I was in no mood to stand and watch as it practiced. I had a deadline of 6 pm to be at the Zeeparel Budget Hotel north of Nieuport and I had no idea where it was.

It was after 4 pm when I reached Nieuport's cathedral. Its vast space was cleverly broken up by clusters of chairs gathered round different statues and icons but I did not feel that I had the time to stop and settle. I swiftly toured the building and headed for the exit, only to find that the day's tropical heat had curdled into a thunder storm. Rain hosed down outside and there was no alternative but to sit beside a statue and ponder my next move. A taxi seemed my best chance of finding the hotel and the town square seemed a good place to find one. I left the cathedral and spotted an elderly lady watching the rain from her shop doorway. When I asked her where I might find a taxi she looked horrified. "Taxi, no!" she declared. "Tram!" Taking my arm, she pointed me to a side street where I would find "Tram!" I did as I was told and walked on through the downpour.

The modern tram station was beside the harbour and its stylish glass and steel canopy offered some protection from the rain. The lady in the ticket kiosk managed to decipher my water smudged print out and gave me a 1.30 Euro ticket to where I needed to go. "Take the Ostend tram and get off at Westende Bad," she instructed. I set off.

Trams are great fun and this one accelerated at speed through suburbs, sand-dunes and scrubland. I enlisted half the passengers around me to identify when Westende Bad appeared and their collective goodwill deposited me in a quiet seaside suburb outside the Catholic church of St Theresa. It had stopped raining and the clear blue sky had returned. It was just after 5 pm but neither I nor the lady in the tram ticket office could see the Zeeparel Budget Hotel. I sought advice from the tourist office. It had closed at 5 pm but there was still someone tidying up inside. She kindly let me in and researched this unfamiliar place. "Oh yes," she said, looking up from her register, "it is on the corner of the next street, right opposite the tram stop."

Thanking her, I rushed back to the street. It was 5.30 pm and I'd been told that the hotel reception closed at 6 pm. I found the Zeeparel Budget Hotel but to my dismay it was locked up and all the lights were off. I stood forlornly gazing at the deserted reception and café before spotting a typed notice stuck on the inside of the plate-glass front door. It had my name on it and a telephone number. I dug out my mobile phone (something I rarely use) and tapped in the numbers.

What happened next felt like a scene from a spy novel. A recorded message burbled at me in a foreign language. I held on. Then a young woman's voice came on the line speaking English. Guiding me around the street corner she said I would see a brown door at the side of the hotel. Beside that door I would see a safe. I found the door and found the safe. "Now," she said, "press the following numbers." I looked over my shoulder, convinced I was being watched but there were no men in raincoats keeping me under surveillance. I pressed the numbers one at a time, slowly. The safe opened. The woman's voice continued: "Inside, you will find an envelope with your name on it. It contains a key to the brown door, a letter and the key to your room. These are your mission instructions. Memorise and destroy them…"

Perhaps I made that last bit up but, as I opened the brown door and crossed the empty hallway to the staircase, it felt like I'd broken into an abandoned building. I entered my room, unslung my rucksack and wedged a chair against the door in case there was a raid.

After a quick shower, I ventured back out. St Theresa's church was open and three people were inside praying quietly. I lit a candle and sat for a while giving thanks for my adventure. I estimated I'd walked 35km since 3.30 am that morning and I had needed every minute to meet my deadline. My shoulders were stiff from carrying the pack but, in all other respects, I was fine. I was also hungry. A quiet, pleasant, no fuss restaurant on the deserted seafront provided the perfect end to a memorable day.

Tea at 'T Hof van de Hemel

CHAPTER FIVE

"Giving every day the chance to be the most beautiful day"

Nieuport, Diksmuide, Markem

Nieuport is where the Western Front meets the sea. On August 3, 1914 Germany invaded Belgium and Britain declared war the next day. German troops advanced swiftly and were soon within range of the coastal ports that they desired. The Belgians and their allies were facing disaster and so they played their final card. On October 29, just 12 weeks after fighting had begun, they opened the great sluice gates that keep the sea out of these coastal low lands. The criss-cross drainage system of canals and ditches now carried the flood water to every corner of the very land they were designed to protect. It was a desperate act, but it succeeded in stopping the huge German army from overwhelming the Belgian, French and British forces. The landscape around Nieuport was transformed. Fields and roads became marshes and lagoons that were impossible for men, horses and equipment to cross. This allowed the defensive line to be shortened and the Allies to concentrate their remaining forces several miles south-east, opposite Diksmuide.

From November onwards, the opposing armies dug in. Lines of trenches soon stretched 450 miles from just north-west of Diksmuide, past Ypres to the French border at Armentières, continuing south and east through the Somme and Verdun before finally ending at the Swiss frontier. For most of the next three years, it was a static landscape, the "great breakthroughs" dreamed of in the Allied offensives of 1915, 1916 and 1917 merely adjusting the line by a few miles in any direction. Even when, in March 1917, the

Germans made a tactical withdrawal to the heavily fortified Hindenburg line they conceded, at most, just 25 miles of territory.

In early 1917, 23-year-old Arthur Gould Lee flew his single seat Sopwith Pup on a Northern Offensive Patrol over this section of the Front from the French mining town of Lens to Diksmuide. He later wrote:

"I gazed down upon the broad band of shell-pitted front lines, looking like the surface of the moon, which emerged from the haze of everything north of Ypres and sprawled under us towards the east of Armentières until it disappeared into the southern horizon. Open for us to inspect were all the secrets of this waste of tortured soil that wound across Belgium and France, a barrier along which millions of armed men crouched in foul trenches, facing each other behind barbed wire, like animals in zoos. Below us lay displayed the zig-zagging entrenchments, the wriggling communications to the rear, the untidy belts of rusty wire in no-man's-land – all the cunningly contrived warrens of trench warfare, which us flyers could examine not only with detachment but with gratitude that we were not there, too."[1]

* * *

For over 50 years I have been reading accounts of life in the trenches and of the exploits of men in the fragile flying machines that flew above them. Like Gould Lee, I read them with detachment and with gratitude that I was not there. However, I also read them with a fascination and wonder. What was it like? How would I have performed if I had been there? What would my fate have been?

I was given Arthur Gould Lee's autobiography for my Applied Maths prize from Holy Cross High School in Hamilton. I already knew a lot about a World War One pilot's life from reading the popular Biggles stories.[2] It was 1970 and, as I read Gould Lee's memoirs, I thought with a young boy's mind that his account was from a history so distant that nothing real could remain.

The following year my father took my sister and me to an air show in Edinburgh. An original Sopwith Pup was scheduled to fly in the same programme as the brand new, futuristic Concorde. Whilst excitedly waiting for the flying to begin I noticed the letters "RFC" on a sign outside a hospitality tent. I couldn't believe that these letters really meant "Royal Flying Corps". Surely there were no real RFC people left alive? I cautiously approached the entrance. "Do you know what RFC stands for?" barked a man guarding the way, his Scots accent harsh, almost sneering. It was as if he was demanding a password. "Royal Flying Corps," I proudly answered, hoping to be granted passage. The bouncer was unimpressed, "This is only for members of the Royal Flying Corps, son," he snapped. "You can't come in."

I was too young to judge age accurately. Everyone older than my parents seemed ancient, so I cannot now say if this man might have served in the RFC himself or whether he was of a slightly younger generation, zealously protecting the holy ground where heroes now gathered. Beyond him in the tent, I could glimpse some men of the RFC, but my opportunity to meet one of them was gone. I still wonder what fascinating conversations I might have had.

As I now prepared for the day's walking from Nieuport, I realised how short a span of time there is in 50 years. The events of 1914–18 felt closer now as I approached my 60th year than they did to me as a boy in 1970. Time takes on a circular, not linear quality and draws me back to those monumental events that are beyond my comprehension yet which, had I lived then, would have been a defining part of my life.

Arthur Gould Lee's Northern Offensive Patrol flight path traced the route I now planned to follow along the old Front Line until it meets the Via Francigena again in Arras. The Western Front is a path that has defined the historical, psychological and, in many ways, the spiritual landscape of the 20th century but it is a landscape that will soon fade from our consciousness. So 2014 perhaps marks the last surge in interest. Those of us whose grandparents were eyewitnesses are now entering our later middle age. In time, the Great War and the Second War will seem as distant as the Napoleonic wars do now.

* * *

The Zeeparel Budget Hotel was as deserted when I left as it had been when I arrived. During the night, the chair I'd wedged against the door had not been disturbed and I'd slept soundly. Back in the centre of town, it took me some time to find the right waterway to follow out of Nieuport. Several converged at the harbour but once I'd found the Ijzer (in French, Yser) river I was reassured by a sign telling me that Diksmuide (Dixmude) was just 18 kilometres along this towpath. Another sign, pointing elsewhere, declared that the Amsterdam to London Way passed here too. I was at an international crossroads for walkers and cyclists.

The river banks were rich in birdlife. Just past St Joris, I noticed a little bird perched on a tall reed growing up from the river bank. He was singing his heart out and, although I was very close, his voice continued so strong and confident that I was able to stop and listen without disturbing him. With no one else around, it was my own private concert. As I walked deeper into the flat countryside, the traffic noise died away and the chorus of calls and conversations between different species became one of the richest and diverse I could remember hearing. A pair of brown backed, black and white winged birds rose up from their nest in the field to my right and began circling me, calling sharply. They clearly considered me a threat and one came so close that, as it cried out, I could see its long, straight bill opening and closing like a filmmaker's clapperboard.

Memorials began to appear that marked different episodes in the early fighting of 1914. The Battle of the Ijzer (Yser) began on October 16 and cost the Belgian army over 20,000 casualties. Such catastrophic losses left the Belgians with only 65,000 soldiers to fight on. There had been no alternative but to open the sluice gates on October 29 and shorten the line of defence. The strategy worked. After the inundation, this relatively small force was able to hold the 18 kilometres between Diksmuide and the sea for the rest of the war.

However, conditions were terrible. The Belgian author, le Goffic, described a forbidding landscape:

> *"Water is everywhere: in the air, on the ground, under the ground. It is the land of dampness, the kingdom of water. It rains three days out of four. The north-west winds which, breaking off the tops of the stunted trees, making them bend as if with age, carry heavy clouds of cold rain formed in the open sea. As soon as the rain ceases to fall, thick white mists rise from the ground giving a ghost-like appearance to men and things alike."*[3]

I was blessed on my walk that morning with warm sunshine and a gentle breeze. Far from forbidding, the landscape looked benign. I paused at a wayside shrine, one of many on my route which housed a simple statue of the Virgin cradling the baby Jesus. Unlike most shrines, it was well cared for with potted flowers in bloom and a candle burning at her feet. I noted the inscription carved into the stone above her head: "GA HER NOO T VOORB O MENSEN VOET ZONDER DAT GY MARIA ERRBIEDIG GROOT."

That evening, my host, Jacques, at De Klaproos bed and breakfast, would struggle to translate it. "It's in an old Flemish dialect," he explained. "Basically, it encourages travellers not to pass this place without saying hello to Mary." I was glad that I had paused and had left my own greeting – a prayer card from my parish of St Anselm's, showing our own mosaic of Our Lady with Jesus in her arms.

* * *

A huge tower, far thicker than a church spire, appeared on the horizon. This was the Ijzer Tower at Diksmuide, Belgium's gigantic, ominous monument to the Great War. Ever since its construction, the Tower has been a place of controversy and conflict and its brooding presence defined the remainder of my walk that morning.

Rain started to fall and it became colder. Amongst some buildings on the other side of the Ijzer river, heads bobbed above a low rampart of concrete sandbags and teenagers with note books scrambled over crumbling concrete pillboxes. I had reached the first fortifications built on the Western Front.

Here, in 1914, the land had begun to emerge from the inundation and military forces once again had the opportunity to manoeuvre. Troops therefore had to "dig in" to defend their ground. Looking across the river now, I could see the tops of heads and an occasional scurrying figure amongst the fortifications. Such were the brief glimpses rival troops gave each other in the Great War as entire communities went about their business virtually underground.

Although just a few yards wide, the river was an effective barrier preventing me from joining the students in their explorations. I assumed that the Ijzer had separated the rival forces during the conflict and, as I faced the Belgian strong point, I assumed the largest bunker at the extreme right of the trenches to be part of their design. However, the exact divide and orientation between Allied and German positions on the Western Front is often confusing. I was amazed to later learn that what I thought was part of the Belgian fortifications facing an enemy across the river was in fact a German bunker with its gun slits aimed at the tip of the Belgian trench just a hundred metres away.

This bunker was at the extreme limit of the German advance. For four years, Belgian soldiers in sodden misery and fear succeeded in holding their remote complex of fortifications against capture. When, on a later visit, I came to stand in those Belgian positions I noticed how their concrete slab walls and gun slits all anticipated an attack from their own side of the Ijzer. Looking across to the enemy bunker, so near and still so menacing, I experienced something of the fear that the soldiers must have felt each day. These rival positions in their remote location at the extreme edge of the Front were intimate, and terrifying. Sudden death was very, very close. Even when manned by visiting school children armed with nothing more than notebooks, a sinister melancholy filled the concrete ruins of the Dodengang – the Trenches of Death.

* * *

On the outskirts of Diksmuide, bridges across the Ijzer allowed me to turn west and re-enter what had been Allied territory. In October and November 1914, the town itself had put up stiff resistance but was captured and remained in German hands throughout the war. After the Armistice, a spot just west of the canal was chosen for the Ijzer Tower, the grandest and most tortured of Belgium's memorials to the conflict. The sign in The Poppy In café where I stopped for lunch assured its customers that "*Love is all you Need*", but the troubled history of the Ijzer Tower reminds visitors just how difficult that is to achieve.

Belgium is a country divided by class and language. It is a rift that goes back to the 18th century when Flemish culture, which had until then been influential throughout Europe, was suppressed by the French speaking regime. The tensions between French and Flemish identity went through many twists and turns but, by the outbreak of the First World War, French was still the only language used in education. As a result, 80% of the officers in the Belgian army were French speakers. The soldiers, however, were predominantly Flemish-speaking and resented their orders being given in French. Germany exploited this division and, in occupying all but one tenth of Belgian territory, nurtured the ambitions of the Flemish speakers. The Flemish University of Ghent was permitted to reopen and ancient grievances against the French speaking Belgians simmered throughout the occupied and unoccupied country.

After the Armistice, the French speaking authorities maintained their control but they could not deny the sacrifices made by the predominantly Flemish speaking army. Diksmuide became a place of pilgrimage and, in 1930, a fifty-metre-high monument was erected to commemorate those who had died on the Ijzer/Yser Front. Although dedicated to peace, it soon became a focus for Flemish nationalism.

Germany's reoccupation of Belgium during the Second World War further fuelled internal tensions. Opponents of Flemish nationalism blew up the Ijzer monument in 1946, justifying its destruction as an act of retaliation for Flemish collaboration with the Nazis. The present, much taller tower was built soon after but neo-Nazi gatherings on the site have contaminated its efforts to be a focus for peace and reconciliation.

The mysterious letters AVV-VVK carved on the thick limbed cross at the very top of the monument stand for the words *"Alles Voor Vlanderen: Vlanders Voor Kristus"* – "All for Flanders: Flanders for Christ". This saying is closely associated with Joe English, a Flemish artist of Irish heritage who, until his death in August 1918, was the Belgian army's official war artist. Joe English was an active member of the Association of Flemish Catholic Students and the AVV-VVK inscription appeared on his controversial design for the headstones of graves of Flemish nationalist soldiers who had been punished for their views by French-speaking officers. These "Joe English" gravestones in the shape of a Celtic cross distinguished them from the official French military crosses which, in the circumstances, Flemish nationalists considered inappropriate for their "martyrs".[4]

The Poppy In café wages its own struggle against cynicism, fear and prejudice with uplifting words framed and hung on its walls. There was a genuine, friendly welcome for a grubby walker with a large rucksack and I soon felt at home in their well-appointed modern furnishings. As I relaxed and ate my meal, I began to think about the clichéd sayings on the café's posters. Clichés, of course, contain a nugget of truth that, when heard for the first time, offer an insight powerful enough to be worth remembering

"Enjoy the little things, one day you look back and realise they were the big things" echoes the wisdom of the religious mystics in urging us to see God in every little thing. *"Give every day the chance to be the most beautiful day in your life"* exhorts the reader to have faith that the underlying, ultimate reality, whatever the state of our lives, is one of love and beauty. To believe in a God of Love is ambitious enough even when life is going well. I wondered how often the troops in the sodden stinking trenches

around here had experienced it. Further on my day's journey, I discovered an answer to that question.

* * *

The footpath continued along the right side of the Ijzer. From time to time, chunks of Great War fortifications could be spotted in the walls of gardens lining the canal's embankment. In the footpath itself, a weathered concrete slab from the roof of a bunker confirmed that I was, literally, walking on the Front Line of the Western Front.

I reached a large, elegant house named Villa Marietta set back at an angle from the canal. A sign told me that this was once the home of Madame Faverger-Tack, a remarkable 78-year-old lady who, during the Great War, had refused to leave her home even though it was just 30 metres from the Front Line. Her daily acts of kindness to the soldiers in the trenches at the bottom of her garden earned her their affection and the title "*Mother of the Soldiers*". In the Ijzer Tower museum there is a short film of Mme Faverger-Tack dressed in long dark skirt and blouse with a medal pinned to her breast. She is stony-faced and sits precariously on a small donkey processing slowly along a trench, greeting soldiers as they work in the shelter of its sandbagged walls.

This remarkable character maintained her stubborn defiance and simple acts of kindness until 1916 when German shelling forced her to move to somewhere safer. Her bravery and her little gifts of fruit, sweets and cigarettes were her way of "giving every day the chance to be the most beautiful day" to soldiers living in terrible conditions where every day might indeed be their last.

* * *

The remains of another Vauban fortress marked the junction of the Ijzer and Ypres canals and I turned here to reach Markem and my accommodation for the night. De Klaproos bed and breakfast provided a delightful self-contained chalet in the back garden of the home of Jacques and his family. For my evening meal, they directed me to a restaurant further along the main road where I could taste something I'd never tasted before.

A recent scandal in the UK had discovered that in some "ready meals" horsemeat was masquerading as beef. I wasn't sure what generated the greater indignation: was it the subterfuge, or the fact that these treasured animals were being eaten? There is no such sentimentality in this part of Belgium. *Paardenbiefstuk,* horsemeat steak, was on the menu and I decided to order it. Like Monsignor Quixote in Graham Greene's novel, I could not tell any difference between the taste of my horse steak and that of beef. With onion gravy, chips, salad and a bottle of Grimbergen beer my *Paardenbiefstuk* dinner that evening slipped down very nicely indeed.

* * *

1. *Open Cockpit,* by Arthur Gould Lee (Jarrolds, 1969) pages 5 and 6. The book was republished by Grub Street in 2018 and quoted here with their kind permission. In early 1917 Gould Lee was flying with 46 Squadron based at La Gorgue, beside the River Lys. In his book, he fondly recalls how he and his colleagues would swim in the river between sorties.
2. Biggles is a fictional character based on the real wartime experience of his creator W E Johns. It is now the fashion to deride Biggles as a symbol of "British Imperialism" but with the First World War stories in particular, W E Johns speaks with an authentic voice of his time. Biggles was a worthy hero to several generations of boys (and a few girls, Fiona included) growing up before and after the Second World War. Our bookshelves at home still creak under the weight of my collection of over 60 titles.
3. Quoted in *Major and Mrs Holt's Battlefield Guide to the Ypres Salient* by Tonie and Valmai Holt (1999 edition), published by Pen & Sword books/ Leo Cooper, page 18 of the Historical Summary, quote reprinted with the publisher's permission.
4. *Ibid*, see page 217 onwards for an excellent overview of the Ijzer Tower's history

The Ijzer (Yser) river

CHAPTER SIX

On Death and Resurrection

Ypres, Hollebeke

Ypres Cathedral, 1930

An organ throbs, its echoes die away,
A shaft of light, rose-tinted, makes a track
That dwells upon an altar breathing peace
I sit, and in my reverie look back...

The walls dissolve, the moonlight filters through,
The stars above shine out in fitful sky,
The altar yawns, the graves again gape wide,
And ghostly voices breathe a murmured sigh.

As in a dream I hear again the sound
Of transport rattle over cobbled street,
The distant drum that tells of lurking death,
And beating pulse of countless marching feet.

A near-by gun booms out its warning note,
I hear the venomed answer whining by,
The earth again is shattered and I hear
A whinny of alarm, and then a cry...

The organ swells, the darkness fades away,
I struggle to the present from the past.
The hum of ghostly voices intertwines
With cadences that breathe of peace at last.

But still there lingers in this town of dreams
Where every stone is sanctified by dead
A breath of English lanes, and hopes of youth.
I sigh and then in silence bow my head.

The scale of slaughter in the Great War is impossible to comprehend. Sir Fabian Ware, founder of what is now the Commonwealth War Graves Commission, observed that, if the British Empire's dead from that conflict were to march four abreast down Whitehall in London it would take them three and a half days, walking day and night, to pass the Cenotaph.[1]

Ypres is a town of ghosts that speaks of death and resurrection. The poem *Ypres Cathedral, 1930* hangs on the wall of the nave in St Martin's cathedral and was discovered amongst the papers of Brigadier General H. M. Hordern OBE, MC. The words capture the spirit of this place for those who served, survived and returned: "I sigh and then in silence bow my head."

The cathedral was destroyed during the conflict but, by the time Hordern made his pilgrimage in 1930, it had been resurrected in its original form. The same was happening across the whole of Ypres. Today we have a vision of an intact medieval town dominated by St Martin's cathedral and the vast Cloth Hall. Both are wondrous replicas of the original constructions from the Middle Ages. The degree of detail in Ypres' complete restoration is astonishing.

My morning's walk from Merkem along the N369 had taken me over the Ypres canal at the point where, in 1914, the British Front Line had crossed to the eastern side of the waterway. This was the most northerly point of an eastward bulge in the trench lines. From here the deviation curved south eastwards, passing (at its closest point) just three kilometres due east of Ypres, before turning south west to where the Line resumed its straight southerly course below the ridge at Messines. For four years soldiers and civilians in this sector were exposed on three sides to fire from German forces dug in on higher ground. This was the "Ypres Salient". Throughout the war, it defined the battleground in what was left of contested Belgian territory.

Ypres[2], together with the Somme, is one of two pivotal points of pilgrimage for Britons, Australians, Canadians, Indians, South Africans and New Zealanders coming to the battlefields today. Here, we try to understand something that is far beyond our comprehension yet unites us by the presence of the Great War in nearly every family history. During these four years, our own humble relatives lived and died alongside those who went on to be defining historic figures of the 20th century. My own great uncle, Arthur John Clark, served in the Ypres Salient as did Winston Churchill, Field Marshal Bernard Montgomery, and Prime Minister Harold MacMillan.

Ypres had to be defended at all costs. A railway brought essential supplies from the Channel ports to Poperinge, 10km west of Ypres and still just out of range of the German guns. If Ypres fell, these supplies would be cut, the way to the ports would be open and the war would be lost.

Ironically, given its later significance, the Germans did actually enter Ypres on October 7, 1914. A force of 20,000 troops took the Burgomaster hostage and exacted a toll of 75,000 francs. However, the Germans soon realised that further advance was impossible. After three days, they left and withdrew several miles to positions on the ridge that ran from Passchendaele in the north east to Messines in the south.

So it was that the Salient was formed and Ypres challenged to hold out. And hold it did. Not only did it withstand the German assaults of 1914, 1915 and 1918 but it also provided the platform for British offensives in 1917 and counterattack in 1918. The Ypres Salient witnessed the full spectrum of brutal innovations devised by military and scientific minds. The flame thrower and poison gas were first used here and mine warfare reached its peak of performance in the 1917 attack on Messines Ridge. Over the course of four years, millions of shells were fired into an area of just 50 square miles. New words for unspeakable horror entered the English language and hell was rebranded with the names of Belgian land marks. None was more terrible than that belonging to the village of Passchendaele – "Passion Dale".

Intense shellfire destroyed the fragile infrastructure that drained the flat farmland around Ypres. When heavy rain fell in the autumn of 1917 the water-table rose and created a swamp of mud. As Allied troops fought their way towards Passchendaele men, animals and machinery were sucked into the ooze as if nature itself was rebelling against the profanity of human destructiveness. This was the Ypres Salient.

* * *

At Pond Farm on the Passchendaele battlefields the Butaye family still plough the land as their forefathers have done for four generations. When the water table freezes each winter, ice churns the soil and pushes solid objects to the surface. It is a potentially lethal harvest.

I'd met the Butaye family some years before when Chris Morgan and I were walking the area where the poet Ivor Gurney had served. We had noticed two massive grey concrete bunkers in a farm yard a hundred metres off to the right that we'd not seen before and went to investigate. At the entrance to Pond Farm there was a well-kept shrine to Our Lady.

Small metal shell casings from the battlefield had been placed beside her statue, but it was the photograph of a sculpted wooden figure of Christ and the story of how it had been found abandoned in 1940 that intrigued us most.

The farm had a private museum which could only be visited during the evening. When we returned at 6 pm, we were welcomed by a young man in his 20s, Stijn Butaye, who had just finished work for the day. Taking us into an old shed beside the barn, Stijn showed us the dozens of Great War artefacts he and his family had discovered whilst working their fields. Outside, in a wire cage in the farm yard, I counted 22 big German high explosive shells and a dozen smaller, sinister gas shells. All had been unearthed over the four months since January and all were potentially lethal.

Stijn showed us a photograph of a column of white smoke rising into the air above a tractor in the field beside their house. His mother had taken the photo a few minutes after Stijn's father, out ploughing the field, had struck a buried phosphorous shell. The shell had exploded under the tractor, releasing toxic chemicals which could have caused fatal burns. The Butaye family were lucky that day. Like many local farmers, their tractor had a reinforced underside to protect the driver from such explosions. Furthermore, the wind was strong and, on that occasion, coming from the right direction to blow the dangerous smoke away from Stijn's father and from the family home.

Campaigns have increased public awareness of the huge number of unexploded mines and bombs that remain from recent wars in Africa and South East Asia. In 1997, Princess Diana, wearing body armour, walked through a minefield in Angola to generate vital funds for those charities working to clear the dangers. However, such campaigns rarely feature the farmers of Belgium who, 100 years after the Great War began, still routinely uncover munitions from their fields. Unexploded shells, even grenades, are often to be seen piled at the foot of telegraph poles waiting for the Belgian army to come and collect them. The national government pays the cost of their destruction, so it is no wonder that Belgians sometimes bitterly remind visitors that other nations fight their wars in their country but leave them to tidy up the mess.

Stijn took us into his house and introduced us to his mother. Over a cup of tea, he told us the story of the hand carved wooden figure of Christ that had been discovered in their farmyard one day in 1940:

"My mother's family have worked this farm for generations. The two huge German bunkers that are still here show how important it was in the First World War, particularly during the Passchendaele battles of 1917. In May 1940, the Germans had broken through and the French armies were retreating. It was chaos. One night, a French cavalry unit rested at the farm. My mum's family hid in one of the bunkers. The French soldiers hurried away the next morning, but they left behind a carved wooden statue of Jesus crucified. My family found it lying on the ground. It had been created with great care, maybe by one of the cavalry soldiers. Jesus seemed particularly helpless lying there. He no longer had his cross and both his arms had gone. The stumps were flung upwards in despair, like the limbs of a disfigured soldier. He shared our feelings as war swept over our fields once again.

"Later, the German soldiers arrived and took over the house and the bunkers. My family slept in haystacks. My mum's grandfather died when his horse was startled by some German soldiers. He was thrown to the ground and died from his injuries. That left my Mum's father, Arsène Marant, to take responsibility for running the farm. He was only 16. Arsène vowed that if he survived the war he would build a shrine for the figure of Jesus that they'd found.

"In 1946, he kept his promise and dedicated a little brick building beside the road to Our Lady of Peace. He wanted that there would be peace in our families and peace among peoples. It was very popular after it was built and pilgrims came from nearby villages to pray at

the shrine. It was said their prayers could be heard by neighbours a kilometre away. We don't get pilgrims now, apart from occasional ones like you. We've taken the figure of Jesus into our house for safe keeping, but you'll see that a statue of Our Lady is kept in the shrine and we look after her every day."

Stijn's mother had brought the wooden carving of Jesus into the kitchen to show us and we felt privileged to be allowed to see and hold their precious family icon. It was a beautiful image, about three feet long, finely sculpted from two pieces of wood sealed together so skilfully I hardly noticed the fault line. The polished, rich brown wood invited you to touch it, to feel the life within the grain. Christ's expression was open mouthed, his cheeks sunken as he gasped for breath. The stumps of his arms were not damaged. Rather, they were the sockets at the shoulder where his arms would have been attached. Perhaps they had been lost, maybe when the figure was detached from its cross, or the artist's work was incomplete and the arms had still to be made.

On the reverse of the statue I could read the letters "EM" carved on Jesus' back together with the date "1940". Here, we had a tantalising clue to the identity of the icon's creator. It is possible he was one of the French cavalrymen who had planned to finish the carving one day. The war had intervened and he was rushed away from the farm to an unknown fate. Did this soldier realise that he had lost his precious prayer, carved from wood? If he did, it would surely have been yet another disappointment amidst the general despair and disaster overtaking him, one more sign that God had deserted him, and the French people. He may have hoped that the icon would be found and respected, but it is unlikely that he could have imagined that over 70 years later it would indeed still be treasured. In that respect, this anonymous cavalryman shared the experience of those who were there when Jesus himself was crucified. In their pain, they could not imagine what good would follow.[3]

* * *

My canal walking ended abruptly at Ypres when the water hit a brick wall beyond which a street continued its line into town. I ate lunch sat on a bench high on the great ramparts that faced east towards the ridge of hills and the old German lines. I felt cold and disheartened by the crowds of people milling around the town. The place felt frenzied and impersonal. Even in the cathedral, there hadn't been anyone to speak to and nowhere to ask for a stamp for my pilgrim's passport. I decided to move quickly on to my next night's accommodation.

Leaving my seat, I walked across to the achingly beautiful little Ramparts cemetery. Here, some 200 graves rested peacefully in a glade of trees on top of the town's broad, high walls. From the cemetery, stone steps took me down to the street to walk out through the Lille Gate, just as countless thousands of soldiers had done 100 years before.

The road skirted Zillebeke Lake, past crumbling British bunkers and the 2,500 soldiers buried in Railway Dugouts cemetery before it began to climb up the side of the ridge that defined the Front Line. A railway running from Ypres disappeared through a deep cutting to my left and I was drawn to signs for Hill 60. Looking back, I could appreciate the significance of this position, just 60 metres above sea level and a mere three or four kilometres from the town. It had not been a long climb, but those few extra metres provided a commanding view of Ypres and all of the flat land around it.

Most battlefield tours will take you to Hill 60, a churned mound of grass covered earth and stone where, early in the morning, sheep can still be found grazing amongst the trees. This was the site of bitter fighting throughout the war and the hill changed hands on several occasions. It was mined and blown up twice and no fewer than five VCs were earned on its slopes. One officer who fought there wrote:

"The place was practically a cemetery, and several hundred men must have been buried on the ground, it proving impossible, when digging trenches, not to disturb some poor fellow in his last long sleep."[4]

Some of those who survived their service on Hill 60 remained deeply connected to this haunting, terrible place. In peacetime, they asked their friends and relatives to grant them one final wish: that when they died, they would have their ashes spread on its slopes.

On the opposite side of the railway cutting from Hill 60 is Battle Wood. Hidden in its midst is the great Caterpillar mine crater, one of a chain of mines exploded simultaneously just after 3 am on June 7, 1917 which launched the Battle of Messines. Much less visited than Hill 60, it is now a secluded and peaceful spot, the bottom of the crater filled with water and its banks fringed with weeping willow.

I had come here once before with Chris Morgan and friends Rupert and Richard Plummer. Rich had researched the Great War stories of his relatives and had long wanted to visit the battlefields. However, this was not an easy journey to make as Rich is a wheelchair user. Our expedition was his only chance to see the places where his family had served. In Battle Wood we had pushed Rich in his wheelchair through the mud and up an overgrown path onto the lip of the mine crater. It was a difficult task but we did not want him to miss this special place. Now, as I stood amongst the weeping willow trees, I felt the strength of our friendship and remembered how we'd celebrated our success, despite the odds, in sharing this little known, almost mystical place with each other.

* * *

My path took me further uphill, across the old German lines and past crumbling concrete fortifications built into the embankment beside the road. I was heading south east, towards the village of Hollebeke and Sans Doute, my bed and breakfast booking for the night.

Sans Doute was in a terrace of two-storey dwellings that ran along one side of a road and looked across to wide open fields on the other. I was early and the little house was all locked up so I walked into the village to buy provisions for my evening meal and to visit the church of Onze-Lieve-Vrouw where I lit a candle of thanks for the day.

The afternoon was wearing on and there was still no sign of the door to my bed and breakfast opening up. I needed to find a toilet, but there wasn't even a discreet bush at the edge of any of the fields opposite the house. I remembered from previous visits to this part of the world that, when designing their churches, Roman Catholics had often been mindful of the needs of male worshippers. I returned to Onze-Lieve-Vrouw and explored the overgrown garden down the side of the building. Sure enough, I found the neglected remains of a *pissoir*, an open roofed chamber of stone with a channel running along one side of the floor. Vegetation grew from cracks in the walls and this softened the functional architecture with a certain style of floral décor. No need for complicated plumbing as the next shower of rain would provide the water to wash out the channel. I was relieved and grateful to the church founders for offering such essential, basic pilgrim hospitality.

* * *

Isabelle came to open up Sans Doute after collecting her children from school. It was a wonderful three-bedroom cottage on two floors and I had it all to myself. That evening I sat in the front yard sheltered by a low fence from the sharp wind blowing across the open fields. The sun was warm on my back and there was hardly any traffic noise to disrupt the birds' evening conversations. Periodically the church bell chimed. It was an idyllic place to sit and write my notes and dine on bread and cheese and ham, with banana, nectarines and yoghurt to follow. Two bottles of Grimbergen blond "certified Belgian Abbey Beer" completed my contentment.

Next morning, I visited the little wayside shrine to Our Lady that stood beside the fields at the end of the street. Unlike most of the shrines I'd passed, it was well cared for and the flame of a burning candle carried recent prayers upwards towards heaven. Some information panels in Flemish were illustrated with a faded photograph of two ordinary middle-aged people standing together in a garden. The man was wearing a dark working coat, like grocers used to wear, over a smart shirt, collar and tie.

The woman beside him wore a floral apron over her blouse and skirt. I was curious to find out more, so I returned to Sans Doute and explained my interest to Isabelle. She was not familiar with the shrine and she kindly agreed to come with me to translate the information panels. The story they told was quite remarkable.

When the German army came again in 1940, Achille Breyne was 44 years old and Secretary to the Mayor. As a local bureaucrat, he had to comply with the new authorities but, in his quiet way, he carried out his acts of resistance. He helped obtain forged identity papers for those who needed them and warned of when the next "work round ups" were scheduled so that some could avoid being pressed into service by the Nazis. In 1943, his deceptions were discovered and he was arrested and transported to Buchenwald concentration camp in Germany.

Achille's wife, Jenny, feared she would never see him again but promised that, if he did return safely, she would make a chapel to Our Lady. When the Americans liberated Buchenwald on April 11, 1945, Achille was amongst the survivors. He returned to the village of Hollebeke in May 1945 and eventually became Mayor himself.

The little shrine we stood in now was made to fulfil Jenny's promise. It was a community effort. A local builder created the rough stone chapel itself, and the tiles for the floor were taken from damaged houses in the village. The local carpenter made the altar and the local stonemason inscribed the dedication above the entrance. The words, when translated, read "Our Lady of Consolation" and are an invitation to all who grieve for those they have lost.

I looked again at the photograph of Achille and Jenny standing together in their garden, wearing their working clothes. If I passed them in the street, I would think there was nothing special about them, perhaps even dismiss them as "unimportant", just as this little shrine is overlooked today. How wrong I would be. I felt humbled by Achille and Jenny (would I have had their courage and resilience?) and privileged that I had discovered their story.

Isabelle confessed that, although she lived just a few yards away, this was the first time she had visited the shrine. She hadn't known anything about its history. Walking back, she pointed to the house beside Sans Doute. "That's where my father lives. I will tell him what I've discovered about the chapel. He enjoys walking like you." A bicycle was secured to the wall of the front yard, a flower box resting on its saddle. "That's my father's," she said. "It's an ornament now. He has walked the Camino to Santiago de Compostela – that's why he has fixed those two white scallop shells to the wheels."

I left Hollebeke feeling that, in the story of the little shrine, I had not only learnt something special but that, as a passing pilgrim, I had been of some value in deepening Isabelle's understanding of where she lived. Such moments are the value of walking, and of walking slowly, and I did not wish to hurry on this fresh and beautiful morning.

* * *

The narrow country road eventually reached the peak of the ridge. Pausing, I gazed at the fields spread out below as they approached the village of Messines (Mesen). There, in the distance, I could see the distinctive shape of a church that had three towers, the middle one bulbous and taller than the others. It looked like a fortress.

Despite the brightness of the sun, the wind began to blow chill. I hunched into my jacket and withdrew into my thoughts. Turning a corner, the land fell away sharply and I was startled by something I did not expect to see. Below me, in this empty landscape, was the white figure of a naked man hanging on a wooden cross. The image was so lifelike that my first reaction was to think, "The poor lad will be freezing." Just for that moment, I was in the immediate presence of an executed criminal left on display by the authorities to deter others from his crimes.

The crucifix has become a familiar image and it has lost its capacity to terrify and disgust. However, outside the confines of a church building, this life-size statue of Christ crucified raised high on a hillside had regained its shocking power.

The familiar account of Christ's trial and crucifixion is read in churches every Easter season. On Good Friday, the account ends when Jesus' body is laid in the tomb, the entrance sealed and the mourners dispersed. It is a bleak narrative. Now, as I looked at this hillside cross on the old battlefields around Messines, the emotional force of that moment in Jerusalem 2,000 years ago struck me. At sunset on that first Good Friday, there was nothing left for Jesus' followers to hope for beyond a future of terrible, unending grief and fear.

If we accept that just the basic facts of the key Gospel events are correct about Jesus' existence, His ministry, and His execution, then something happened in a remarkably short period of time to fundamentally change His followers' bleak despair into prophetic hope. What should have been the end of the story was not. What could have happened that had such power to transform so many lost and broken individuals?

Asking, or being asked, "Do you believe in God?" begs the question: "It depends what you mean by God." It's a discussion that can too easily slip off into complex intellectual arguments, or lightweight appeals to feelings or instinct. The question "What changed the apostles?" is much more powerful and leads to richer enquiry. It has its basis in real, lived experience.

Common sense explanations, like the loss of the body or a medical recovery from shock induced coma, do not have the power to inspire Jesus' terrified followers to do what they went on to do. A lost body would only add to the enduring grief of His family and friends, not revitalise them. Recovery after crucifixion would be remarkable, but the brutal scourging that took place before nails were hammered through hands and feet would cripple the man for the rest of his life. He would be pitied and cared for, but not followed.

More contrived, though still plausible, are theories of conspiracy to steal the body and introduce a substitute to miraculously appear soon afterwards. However, these too struggle to answer the key question "What transformed the disciples?". Clever tricks make us wonder, but do they fundamentally change us? Could such a trick ever be the driving force for the influential and energetic movement that began preaching in Jerusalem just seven weeks after their leader had been executed there? [5]

As I stood by that wayside cross, I concluded that I knew the answer to what did not happen after Jesus' body had been taken down from the cross. Therefore, what remained to explain the transformation of those who had been there on that first Good Friday was what they themselves said had happened, what they called Jesus' "Resurrection from the Dead", his tangible presence beyond death. Although it is beyond my comprehension, I could not dismiss it as untrue.

* * *

1. Quoted in an article by Esther Addley in *The Guardian* newspaper November 12, 2018.
2. The town is best known by its French name, Ypres, but its official name appears on signposts in Flemish as Ieper. To this day I still misread it as "Leper" and consider it an apt acknowledgement of the town's maimed and mutilated identity.
3. After our first visit in 2011, I wrote an article for the *Catholic Herald* telling Ivor Gurney's story and that of the little chapel at Pond Farm. Stijn had excitedly emailed me that, as a result of the article, the Pond Farm museum's website www.depondfarm.be/en/themuseum had received 100 new visits and he thanked me for telling their story. When I visited again in 2014, I was honoured to see the article carefully framed and hanging amongst the shell casings and equipment that he and his family had recovered from their fields.
4. See *Major and Mrs Holt's Battlefield Guide to the Ypres Salient*, by Tonie and Valmai Holt, Pen & Sword Books/ Leo Cooper, page 111 quoted with the publisher's permission.
5. The rational arguments that seek to explain the Resurrection are not explored as often or as thoroughly as they should be. It is the central event in Christianity and deserves rigorous debate before any conclusions,

natural or supernatural, are drawn. Anglican Bishop Hugh Montefiore's *The Womb and the Tomb* (Fount, 1992); *The Resurrection* by the Jewish scholar, Geza Vermes (Doubleday, 2008) and *The Jesus Inquest* (Monarch Books, 2008) by the barrister Charles Foster are among the books I've found most helpful.

Jesus of Pond Farm

CHAPTER SEVEN

The Christmas Truce

Messines to Armentières

The road slipped and twisted through open fields and down the hillside, entering Messines from what had been the German side of the lines. The village and its church stand on an ancient route along the Messines Ridge with commanding views of the surrounding landscape. It was 12.30 pm and, as I arrived, St Nicolas' carillon of 15 bells chimed the Prayer of St Francis, "*Make me a channel of your peace...*"

The church door was open and I entered the cool dark space. Candles flickered beneath a statue of Our Lady and the smell of incense lingered in the air. I had visited this church many times over the years and had sometimes joined the small congregation for the Saturday evening Vigil Mass, but today I was alone.

The church of St Nicolas at Messines is the most sacred of places, a small piece of ground where I sense, most acutely, the powerful forces of good and evil that have struggled not only for its own soul, but for the very faith and hope of humankind. Let me try and explain.

* * *

When the German army settled its line of defence along this ridge in 1914, they occupied an extensive complex of religious buildings at the heart of the village of Messines. Founded in 1060 by Adela of France (the mother of William the Conqueror's wife, Matilda of Flanders), the great Abbey with its school and orphanage reflected the prosperity of the farm lands around it. It was a superb vantage point from which the ground sloped sharply down some 200 feet or so before levelling out across a mile of open fields to the hamlet of St Yvon and Ploegsteert Wood where the British lines were drawn.

By December 1914, the war had reached a stalemate. Everyone now realised that, despite those early predictions, the fighting would not be over by Christmas. In the ruins of St Yvon, Lt Bruce Bairnsfather watched the sun fade on Christmas Eve afternoon. The sky was clear and he felt *"a sense of strangeness in the air."* There was no shooting, and he thought:

"It was just the sort of day for peace to be declared. I came out of my dugout and sloshed along the trench to a dry lump, stood on it and gazed at all the scene around: the stillness, the stars, and the now dark blue sky. From where I stood, I could see our long line of zigzagging trenches and those of the Germans as well. Songs began to float up from various parts of our line." [1]

The recently elected Pope Benedict XV had appealed for a Christmas ceasefire but the authorities on both sides rejected the notion as impossible. However, what happened as the sun slowly set on that Christmas Eve was remarkable, if not miraculous. Despite the wishes of all those in the German, British, French and Belgian high command, soldiers on both sides took part in spontaneous, peaceful initiatives along the length of the Western Front. What became known as "The Christmas Truce" began on the German side of the lines.

The mood that Lt Bairnsfather noticed on Christmas Eve afternoon had, in fact, begun to weave its spell the night before. The Germans had already moved Christmas supplies from stores in the ruins of Messines to their front line at the foot of the ridge. After dark on the 23rd, Saxon soldiers from Leipzig began placing small Christmas trees, *Tannenbaum*, on the parapets of their trenches. Candles were clamped to the branches and these now began to cast a flickering, fascinating light across the blasted landscape.

British soldiers from the Berkshire regiment began to crawl out of their trenches, curious to find out about these mysterious lights. No shots were fired. Instead, those Saxons who could speak English called out that these *Tannenbaum* were more important than the war and that nothing could stop them celebrating Christmas Eve among their traditional trees.

Soon officers on both sides were in contact with each other. The war itself had gone quiet in this sector and the rows and rows of glittering *Tannenbaum* encouraged the British to believe that the Germans' desire to celebrate a peaceful Christmas was genuine. Both sides agreed to observe an informal truce on Christmas Eve and Christmas Day. If nothing else, it would allow them all to bury their dead.

At St Yvon, the opposing armies' trenches were only a few yards apart across a waterlogged turnip field. Bairnsfather recalled:

> *"I woke at dawn and on emerging on all fours from my dugout became aware that the trench was practically empty. I stood upright in the mud and looked over the parapet. No Man's Land was full of clusters... of khaki and grey...pleasantly chatting together. Cigarettes and other souvenirs were being exchanged, and there was talk of football matches later in the day."*[2]

Bairnsfather joined in and, despite language difficulties, he and a German lieutenant agreed to swap buttons from their tunics.

> *"I brought out my wire clippers, and, with a few deft snips, removed a couple of his buttons...I gave him two of mine in exchange."*[3]

High up on the ridge, among the ruins of Messines, soldiers of the Bavarian regiment could see their comrades mixing with the British. They had celebrated Christmas Eve night in what remained of the old Abbey, singing "Stille Nacht". One of them, Private Rupert Frey, had marvelled as *"the high and gloomy monastery walls vanished, and we saw only the sparkling Christmas tree."* Now they debated whether to go down and join their enemies in No Man's Land. In the cellar of the old monastery, one soldier, nicknamed "Adi" by his colleagues, was adamant that this was wrong: *"Such a thing should not happen in wartime,"* he told them. *"Have you no German sense of honour left at all?"*[4]

Private Adolf Hitler had already earned the Iron Cross, second class, for his courage in rescuing a wounded officer. Although baptised a Catholic, he had refused to take part in any form of religious observance during the Christmas period. When a Lutheran theology student, Corporal Frobenius, read the Christmas Gospel to a joint congregation of Catholics and Protestants, Rupert Frey observed that "Adi" was absent.

Not surprisingly, Hitler's views were shared by senior officers in the British, French, Belgian and German armies, as well as by many of the soldiers themselves. In some places, the truce lasted until New Year but sniping and shelling, often by different regiments to those who had met each other in No Man's Land, began again once Christmas had passed. Tighter discipline and the increasingly bitter fighting meant that there was no repeat of the Christmas Truce in the years that followed.

Bairnsfather himself ruefully commented:

"It was too much to expect that a table would be suddenly wheeled out into No Man's Land, accompanied by English and German Ministers with fountain pens and documents, ready to sign 'peace'."

With the passing of the Christmas holiday, he watched as *"bullets whizzed around that one-time meeting place (between the lines), and sundry participants in that social gathering were laid out stiff on parapets, awaiting burial."*[5]

However, the experience of meeting the enemy, and realising that they were ordinary, quite decent men like themselves had a profound impact on those who had taken part. Private Rupert Frey, who had come down from his shelter in the Abbey, wrote that they had gathered *"as if we were friends, as if we were brothers. Well, were we not, after all!"*[6]

The informal Christmas Truce of 1914 was often played down by the military authorities. Indeed, as the years progressed, the events seemed so remarkable that many began to wonder if they were, in fact, just a fanciful myth. However, the weight of documented evidence is compelling and such doubts no longer exist. On the edge of the turnip field at St Yvon, a wooden cross now stands as a symbol of hope, commemorating when, in the words of another witness of the 1914 Truce, Kurt Zehmisch, *"Christmas, the celebration of Love, managed to bring mortal enemies together as our friends for a time."*[7]

* * *

During his time in Messines, Adolf Hitler painted a watercolour of the ruined church and copies of it survive to this day. He was a reasonable architectural artist and this was one of Hitler's favourite paintings. Some say that, once he was in power, he had it hung in his office in Berlin.

In June 1917, the British detonated a chain of mines along the ridge in a terrifying and effective opening to the Battle of Messines. British and Empire forces swept through the German defences before grinding to a halt in the mud of Passchendaele beyond. Fighting over the ridge continued through 1918 and, by the end, Messines and its ancient abbey were totally obliterated. Even the ruins that Hitler had painted were completely destroyed. The Church of St Nicolas was the only part of the abbey to be reconstructed after the war. The original design was followed as much as possible, especially the distinctive bulbous bell tower that makes it such an unusual landmark today.

Some of the original cellars and foundations were preserved in the reconstruction. As I walked further into the church, I noticed a small door to the right of the altar. Opening it, I followed a winding staircase down into the crypt. The small underground chamber with its vaulted ceiling was a gloomy place, the only daylight coming from two little windows high up in its east wall. I shivered in the chilled air as even with the midday sun shining through there was no warmth in that space. Cobwebs hung from the rows of arched brick pillars dividing the crypt into three bays. In the middle one, a stone slab marked the grave of Adela of France herself. Buried here in 1079, she has been a silent witness to all that has happened since.

During 1914, the Germans used this crypt as a field hospital and medics treated Adolf Hitler here for a wound to his arm. It was a curious thing to stand in this place where the air is always cold and to know that, when he was here, Hitler was just an unimportant, thin-faced soldier nicknamed "Adi", an ordinary man before his name became so comprehensively associated with evil.

In June 1940, whilst British forces were evacuating from Dunkirk and French soldiers were still fighting to hold as much of their country as they could, Hitler came to survey his conquests. It was his supreme moment and movie cameras followed him driving in state through Paris on June 23 and earlier, on June 1, walking through the Menin Gate at Ypres. In Belgium, he reinforced his reputation as a battle-hardened veteran of the Great War by revisiting the scenes of his own military service. From Ypres, he drove to Messines and stopped near the rebuilt church he'd known so well. Getting out of his car, Hitler walked towards St Nicolas' great west doors. As he approached, a local man, a caretaker of the church, turned his back and ignored him. Hitler's aides were furious and made to seize the man and teach him a lesson. However, Hitler was enjoying the occasion and, in a surprising moment of compassion, he told them *"No, leave him alone. He has every right to be angry with us."*[8]

Hitler had returned to reclaim his memories and to rewrite the bitterness of the defeat he had felt in 1918. That bitterness had driven him on and had provided the power behind the hate unleashed again in 1939. Hitler's visit of 1940 brought his spirit back to this place, contaminating its holy ground. In the years since, others have successfully reclaimed St Nicolas of Messines as a beacon of peace and reconciliation. In 1967, Otto Meyer, a German veteran who'd fought near here in the First War, presented St Nicolas with a copper chandelier, "The Rose of Messines", as a symbol of peace. Eighteen years later, donations from all over the world paid for a carillon of 15 bells to be made in time for the historic visit of Pope John Paul II on May 17, 1985 to Ypres. The Pope, who as a young man had lived under Nazi rule in Poland, blessed the first of the bells that now chime the half hour from St Nicolas' bell tower.

Pope John Paul's blessing, and Otto Meyer's gift have helped exorcise the evils that Messines has witnessed. St Nicolas is a holy place, tested by some of the most terrible events in history. Lighting a candle in this heavy, brooding church, I was forced again to ponder, as I had that morning in the shrine erected by the Breyne family in Hollebeke, the potential of ordinary, insignificant people just like me to do great deeds of good, and of evil. When he was serving at Messines in 1914, "Adi" Hitler was still an ordinary soldier and not yet the monster he became.

* * *

The road to France from Messines ran down the hillside towards the British lines and Ploegsteert ("Plugstreet") Woods. Behind me, the 110 foot tall Irish Peace Tower looked down from the ridge, commemorating a time when Protestant and Catholic Irishmen fought side by side in the 1917 assault. The Tower was erected in 1998, and dedicated on November 11th that same year by Britain's Queen Elizabeth II, the Irish president, Mary McAleese and Belgium's King Albert II. The monument and the Peace Park that surrounds it sought to draw strength from the events of 1914–18 to cement the fragile peace then emerging in Northern Ireland. The Good Friday Agreement to end 30 years of sectarian conflict had been signed in April and hopes were high that a conflict that had seemed unending was now over. The Peace Pledge unveiled by the dignitaries that November day in 1998 captured this new spirit of penance and reconciliation. It read:

"From the crest of this ridge, which was the scene of terrific carnage in the First World War on which we have built a peace park and Round Tower to commemorate the thousands of young men from all parts

of Ireland who fought a common enemy, defended democracy and the rights of all nations, whose graves are in shockingly uncountable numbers and those who have no graves, we condemn war and the futility of war. We repudiate and denounce violence, aggression, intimidation, threats and unfriendly behaviour.

"As Protestants and Catholics, we apologise for the terrible deeds we have done to each other and ask forgiveness. From this sacred shrine of remembrance, where soldiers of all nationalities, creeds and political allegiances were united in death, we appeal to all people in Ireland to help build a peaceful and tolerant society. Let us remember the solidarity and trust that developed between Protestant and Catholic Soldiers when they served together in these trenches.

"As we jointly mark the armistice of 11 November 1918 – when the guns fell silent along this western front – we affirm that a fitting tribute to the principles for which men and women from the Island of Ireland died in both World Wars would be permanent peace."

Inside the stone tower, volumes of Registers lined the circular wall, recording, in alphabetical order, the names of Irish soldiers who served in the Great War. I counted 114 with the name "Dunne", their records covering eight pages of the Register. Most were from Dublin, a few from County Kilkenny where my closest relatives now live, but I could see none from the town of New Ross, in County Wexford, where my father, Michael Bernard Dunne, was born just after the war. [9]

* * *

I strode on down the road. In Ploegsteert village itself, a plaque recorded Winston Churchill's front-line service here in 1915–16. Churchill had come to redeem himself after being humbled as First Lord of the Admiralty by the failure of his plan to land an army in the Dardenelles to capture Constantinople. The Gallipoli campaign was a disaster and Churchill took the blame. After he was sacked, he opted for front-line service to make amends and he came here to command the 6th Battalion of the Royal Scots Fusiliers. Despite his tarnished reputation, he won respect and affection from those he commanded. One wrote:

> *"No man was ever kinder to his subordinates, and no commanding officer I have ever known was half so kind... We came to realise his tremendous ability."* [10]

Beyond Ploegsteert, I skirted the French border to go west round Armentières and head for Nieppe. It promised a shorter route to my accommodation for the night. Huge rain clouds threatened and the panorama across the flat fields back towards Belgium was dramatic. From the spire of Ploegsteert church to my left I could see all the way round to Mount Kemmel and the hills beyond to my right. I walked quickly on to the hamlet of La Clef de Hollande, "the key to Holland", a pivotal name for such a humble little place. "Capture this," I could hear the generals say across the ages, "and all the Flemish lands are ours."

I found the tow path alongside the River Lys where Arthur Gould Lee and his RFC comrades had once bathed and followed it past the concrete British pillboxes built to repel any attack from across the river. This threat materialised in April 1918 when General Ludendorff's Spring Offensive swept across the Lys' natural line of defence. Armentières was occupied, Messines and the Passchendaele Ridge retaken and, once more, Ypres threatened to fall.

The outcome of the First World War was in the balance but by the end of the month the German initiative was faltering. They failed to take Ypres and the way to the Channel ports remained closed. From August, British, French, Belgian and American forces attacked across the whole length of the Western Front winning battle after battle to push the German line right back through Belgium and France to the border with Holland in the north and to Germany itself in the south.

On August 2, 1918, in the preliminary stages of what became known as the Hundred Days Offensive, my great uncle, 28-year-old Gunner Arthur John Clark, service number 45644, was *"killed in action in the Advance"*. Arthur had volunteered in 1914 and arrived at the Front in August 1915 where he served with 11ᵗʰ Royal Field Artillery in *"numerous engagements"*[11]. We do not know exactly where he was serving around Ypres when he was fatally wounded but there was time to transport him back to the great field hospital at Lijssenthoek, just west of Poperinge, before he succumbed to his injuries. Arthur was buried in the hospital grounds where his grave is tended to this day.

* * *

I discovered that there are not many footbridges across the Lys. To cross the river, I had to climb the bank of a road bridge and walk carefully along its narrow sidewalk to reach my destination for the night. Le Clos de Flanders at Erquinghem-Lys offered accommodation in converted farm buildings of regal proportions. My ground floor room looked out through huge tall windows onto a central yard. The ceiling was high, the double bed vast and the furniture antique. Mme Decornet provided homemade cakes for breakfast but no evening meal. She told me that there were places to eat nearby but I had not seen any as I stumbled along the narrow path beside the busy main road. With fields all around, Le Clos de Flandres seemed remote. It had been a long day and I figured I'd walked at least 25 kilometres from Hollebeke. I didn't fancy a long search for a place to eat. So, with my diary open in front of me, I sat at a fine writing desk with inlaid wood patterns and unpacked what food I had collected on my way.

Dinner that evening consisted of half a fresh baguette from a baker in Pont de Nieppe (but without butter), a triangle of cream cheese from my breakfast at Sans Doute, my final handful of the apricots that Fiona had given me in London and the last cherry tomato from the packed lunch Chris Morgan had prepared for me on Monday morning. In my room there was a kettle and some Lipton's breakfast teabags, so I settled to my feast and gave thanks for those who had provided it.

That evening, I wrote with some pride that I had covered 120km over four days' walking from Dunkirk along the length of the old front line in Belgium to the French border at Armentières. Next day, I planned to take a bus back to Messines to attend Mass at 6 pm in St Nicolas. Chris Morgan had promised to meet me there with his car at 7pm. I was looking forward to having his company.

* * *

1. *Silent Night* by Stanley Weintraub, published by Simon & Schuster UK, 2001, pages 18–19. Bruce Bairnsfather became famous as the War's most popular cartoonist, his much-loved Old Bill character capturing the essence of British humour amidst all the horror. All quotes are reprinted with the kind permission of the publishers.
2. *Ibid* pages 90–91.
3. *Ibid* page 99.
4. Over 30 years later, Rupert Frey's account was published in a history of his regiment, *Becoming Brothers between the Fronts: Four Years at the Western Front. The History of the Regiment List. 16th R.J.R.*, edited by Fridolin Solleder, trans. by Beate Engel-Doyle (Munich 1952) – quoted in Weintraub *op. cit.* pages 46 and 79
5. *Silent Night*, page 176.
6. *Ibid* page 163.
7. *Ibid* page 119.
8. As told by historian Steve Douglas in *Private Hitler's War 1914–1918* a 2014 DVD documentary from Beckmann Visual Publishing. During Douglas' voiceover, the film shows a photograph of Hitler with two of his aids standing, caps in hand, inside a church. Alas, they are not at Messines, but in Laon Cathedral which they visited later in their tour, on June 25, 1940.
9. I have not heard any family stories of Irish great uncles joining up in 1914–18. However, in 1942, my father decided to leave his studies and join the British forces. His two older brothers, Paddy and Philip, made the same decision. When I'd asked him why he did it, my Dad had shrugged his shoulders. "It was an adventure," he said. Happily, none of them paid a price for their adventure. Philip and Dad trained as ground crew in the RAF and Dad's posting to Egypt came after the conflict had been settled in that part of the world. My Uncle Paddy joined the army and served in India

in the pay corps. These were jobs that needed to be done, but they were not the jobs that featured in the Sunday afternoon war films of my childhood. Then, I was a little bit disappointed. Now, I am relieved and most grateful.

10. Major A D Gibbs, quoted in *Major and Mrs Holt's Battlefield Guide to the Ypres Salient* by Tonie and Valmai Holt (1999 edition), published by Pen & Sword books/Leo Cooper page 189 and quoted with their kind permission.

11. As recorded in the *National Roll of the Great War 1914–1918*, Section V, Luton, page 70.

Live shells at Pond Farm from the Passchendaele battlefield

Part Two – October 2014

Fromelles, Loos, Lens, Arras, Albert, the Somme, Péronne, Clastres, Laon

Laon Cathedral:
"Around the deep porches of the three west doors, a crowd of sculpted life-size figures stood just a few feet above the ground. Each one's character was clear to see and it was as if they were welcoming us personally."

CHAPTER EIGHT

Jack and Henry

Fromelles, Douvrin, Loos, Lens

Fiona and I did not realise how fortunate we were to be resuming the walk during France's school term-time. Getting to Lille by Eurostar was easy, but getting back on the route was more complicated. This section of the walk would finish at Laon. We had limited time and limited walking capacity, so the best calculation we could make was to find a bus from Lille that would take us just south of Armentières to Fromelles where we would rejoin the line of the Western Front.

The tourist information office guided us to the Lille Metro which took us to the 235 bus waiting outside Oscar Lambret station. It was late morning and the bus was setting off on its lunch time mission to collect students from country schools and bring them home. The bus does not run when the schools close outside of term-time so we understood how lucky we were to be enjoying coffee and cake in the pleasant little café beside Fromelles church at 12.30pm. We had made excellent time.

There was much to reflect on at Fromelles as we prepared for this next stage of the walk. Just south of here, in May 1915, the British had attacked German positions on Aubers Ridge incurring heavy casualties for no territorial gain. For a year after, this section of the line was considered relatively quiet until, in July 1916, Fromelles was chosen for an attack by British and Australian troops. The plan was to divert German attention and resources away from the fighting on the Somme some 70 kilometres or so further south. The Fromelles attack lasted just 12 hours and was another disaster. The Australians were taking part in their first major assault of the war and suffered an astonishing casualty rate of close to 90%. It was a resounding victory for the Germans, who repelled the attack from solidly constructed concrete bunkers that still mark the battlefield to this day. Adolf Hitler served as a messenger in this area and he was proud of his part in the fighting. After he visited Messines in June 1940, he was keen to motor on to revisit the bunkers that he had known so well.

Many of the bodies of those who died on the battlefield were lost. However, in 2018, the remains of 250 Allied soldiers were found in a mass grave in Pheasant Wood, near Fromelles. German troops had probably buried the bodies quickly to prevent disease and their discovery now led to the decision to create the first new Commonwealth War Graves cemetery in 50 years. Furthermore, there was also the opportunity to use modern scientific techniques to try to identify each individual.

In Australia, adverts invited relatives of those who might have died at Fromelles to come forward. DNA samples were taken and these were cross-referenced with DNA from the bones of the dead. From this, 96 Australian soldiers were identified and their relatives had the comfort of knowing that they were lost no more.

After paying our respects at the new cemetery, we set off on the road leading out of the village towards Herlies. We could see two of the old front line bunkers in the flat fields off to our right as we walked on through the villages of Herlies, Marquillies and Salomé. A sign for German cemeteries at Wicres reminded us that this part of France, well behind the German front line, would have been a mystery to Allied troops looking out from their posts across No Man's Land.

A pedestrian footbridge of rusting industrial iron took us across the L'Ancre Canal. A few yards to our left, traffic rushed across the busy modern bridge but we lone walkers seemed to be in a different world of time and pace, of flaking paint and growing weeds.

That evening, as we sat with a beer at the very pleasant Le Colibri hotel, I reflected on the day and regretted that I had not asked the museum at Fromelles cemetery to stamp our pilgrim passports. I had been keen to get walking again, but I now felt that we had failed to properly mark the start of this stage of the walk. However, I had stopped long enough at the museum to buy a couple of pens and now, sorting through my pockets, I looked again at the receipt I had been given. Below the figures for my payment and after the standard corporate thanks for my custom from the *"Musee de la bataille de Fromelles"*, I noticed four words which surprised me: *"Sainte Thérèse d'Avila"*. It seemed that the start of our journey had been blessed after all, by a 16th century Spanish Carmelite mystic.

* * *

Next day the sun was shining. We walked through the side streets of Douvrin towards a bright green water tower marking footpaths that led out of town across the neighbouring fields. Here a group of primary school children were gathered quietly with their teacher as she encouraged them to listen to the birdsong all around them. The little ones were silent, focused and I felt mischief afoot. "Good morning!" I called out cheerily as we passed. Immediately, the spell was broken. "Hallo, hallo!" came several young voices excitedly adding to each other like the sound of water rushing over rocks. "Hallo, hallo!" I grinned and waved but made sure I did not catch the eye of the teacher whose lesson I'd now taken way off course. The English fools tramped briskly on with lively little French voices calling after us "Bye, bye, bye, bye" until we were completely out of sight.

We had a network of paths to choose from. One followed the embankment of a lost railway line, but we chose another which ran along the side of a huge field of maize. Its crops were as tall as us but, surprisingly, the corn cobs were unharvested and turning black with rot. It seemed a great waste. Emerging from behind the crops, we could see the village of Hulloch ahead across open fields. To our left, the peaks of two giant conical coal slag heaps several hundred feet tall dominated the horizon. This was coal mining country and these two manmade mountains rising up from the flat lands, the Double Crassier, provided the defining images of another of 1915's bloody battles. From these vantage points, the

German troops had looked down over British lines to the north and east, their machine gun posts guarding the road to the important town of Lens behind them. The small village just to the north, Loos-en-Gohelle, gave the battlefield its name, one that is again remembered for its disastrous outcome and for the death of the son of one of the British Empire's greatest voices.

* * *

Once the war of movement had settled into the rigid trench lines of the Western Front, the German armies were content to hold and reinforce their positions. Normally this was on the highest ground available to give them tactical advantage. The onus lay with the French and British forces to drive the invader out. Britain had made its first organised assault at Neuve Chapelle and then at nearby Aubers Ridge in the spring of 1915. As autumn approached, the Allies made plans for an even greater assault. The French would launch a huge attack in the Champagne and Artois regions and, to support it, Britain would seek to break through the line at Loos. If successful, Lens and the valuable coal fields surrounding it would open up before them. The British commander, General Haking, rallied his officers on September 24 with the observation that, *"We are on the eve of the biggest battle in the history of the world."*[1]

It was indeed Britain's biggest initiative thus far in the war. Six divisions (about 108,000 officers and men) were assembled to attack the three German divisions dug in around Loos. The technology of war was already developing rapidly. Aircraft were now playing a significant role in aerial observation and poison gas had become available as a terrifying means to dislodge soldiers from their defensive positions. Significantly, the profile of Britain's serving soldiers had changed too. Many of the experienced troops who had arrived in France in August 1914 had perished in the fighting that followed. Filling the ranks were the enthusiastic recruits who had volunteered at the outbreak and who had now completed their training. Loos was to be their first big battle and among them was 18-year-old Second Lieutenant John Kipling, the only son of Carrie and Rudyard Kipling.

* * *

The village of Hulloch disappointed us. There was neither café nor shop to buy refreshment, just a hairdresser's and a locked-up church. Beyond it, there were more wide flat fields. The sun still shone, but now there was nothing to break the strong wind coming into our faces from the west. This was no breeze. This was an elemental force which, even on this most mild of days, demanded we engage and push ourselves forward against it.

We crossed the road that runs south-west from Hulloch to Loos-en-Gohelle which had been an important boundary when the battle began on September 25, 1915. By crossing it, we moved from German territory into the British zone of attack. The British strategy was to use the wind that we could now feel in our faces to carry poison gas into the German lines. The Germans had used gas with deadly success near Ypres in April and now Britain intended to use it for the first time here.

British hopes were high of achieving an immediate breakthrough when the attack was launched at 6.30 am. On the southern part of the battlefield, where we now stood, the wind blew as planned towards Loos and the German lines. However, a few kilometres to our right, to the north of the road running east/west between Hulloch and the village of Vermelles, the wind changed direction and blew the gas back onto the advancing troops. It caused mayhem and the advance stalled.

Second Lieutenant John Kipling, with the 2nd Battalion of the Irish Guards, arrived on the battlefield on September 27, the third day of fighting. Like many of his comrades, this was Kipling's first taste of battle. He had enthusiastically joined up the year before, despite having extremely poor eyesight and needing to wear glasses all the time. Still just 18 years of age, Kipling had grown a moustache to make himself look older to the men under his command. At 4 pm, his unit was ordered to advance across the Hulloch to Loos road, attack a chalk pit and what remained of a nearby wood, before moving on to take the buildings over a mine head known as *Puits 14 bis*. The distance was several hundred yards, but the regiment's War Diary recorded that by 5 pm they had reached a point *"just beyond the PUITS building."*[2] It was here that Kipling was seen to be wounded. By the end of the day he was formally reported as missing.

Our friend Chris Morgan had given us his well-used walking map on which he'd traced the trench lines of 1915. For two kilometres, we followed a long straight farm track that had once been "Gun Trench" until we reached the edge of the village of Loos itself. Tracking through the bungalows and past a modern, life-sized crucifix we turned right to leave the houses behind us and begin the climb towards the ridge that runs right to left across the open fields. British troops had advanced down this slope towards the German defences in the village we were now leaving. Far to our left, trucks thundered along the busy N43 but here, in these open fields we were once again in the different world of the lone walker. There was time and space and peace to engage the spirit of the place.

Beyond an isolated cluster of trees, we could see a structure with high stone walls, crowned with four white domes, two either side of a brilliant white crucifix. The building had the square, solid character of a frontier fort, its domes giving it an exotic Byzantine quality. It reminded me of a remote Coptic convent I had once visited on the edge of the Egyptian desert. Trudging up a grey muddy track we were fascinated by this vision, glimmering white, transported from another world.

The mysterious structure was Dud Corner, the biggest cemetery on the Loos battlefield. At the entrance, we climbed up above the walls to an observation platform and looked back across the fields where we had walked and to the Double Crassier beyond. The view was superb. British commanders pinned down by murderous fire from the monstrous slag heaps would have craved such a vantage point. Looking at the Double Crassier today, I thought of Tolkien's Mordor and its Mountains of Doom. These too had guarded the gateway to hell.

Like many of the Great War's memorials, Dud Corner Cemetery was built on the site of a German strong point and had been a focus for the killing all around. The cemetery's fortress walls now protect the graves within and carry the names of over 20,500 soldiers with no known resting place. Among them is the name of Second Lieutenant John Kipling. When Rudyard and his wife Carrie heard that John was missing, they had clung to the hope that he might have been captured and be recovering in a German hospital. They made great efforts to find those who had survived the battle to try to piece together a picture of John's last known hours. In time, they came to accept that he had not survived and that his body was lost in the chaos and destruction of the battlefield. Like so many grieving parents, the Kiplings were devastated, but stoical. In writing to a friend, Rudyard took comfort in reports that John had acted bravely in battle:

"It was a short life. I'm sorry all the years' work ended in one afternoon but – lots of people are in our position – and it is something to have bred a man." [3]

The search for John's body continued long after the Kiplings themselves had passed away. In 1992 it was decided that the grave of an unknown Lieutenant of the Irish Guards was in fact that of John Kipling. The headstone was reengraved and it is visited now as John's memorial. However, subsequent research has fundamentally questioned the evidence for this decision [4] and so attention is once again turning to his name on the memorial of the missing at Dud Corner Cemetery.

The Loos battlefield feels raw. It is a bleak, flat landscape dominated by the same huge slag heaps that the soldiers fought over in 1915. Visitors are few and those that come usually just pull in off the main road at Dud Corner Cemetery, climb the observation tower, read the information boards and move on. That day, there was no café, no visitor centre, no tour groups, just us, the wind and the Double Crassier. We walked on towards Lens, the trucks rushing uncomfortably close beside us. The path promised tedious, functional walking through the outskirts of town. We spotted a bus stop and discovered that a bus was due within half an hour. It was an easy decision to make.

* * *

The battle of 1915 was the last time that Loos featured prominently in the great narrative sweep of the First World War. The Somme in 1916, and Passchendaele in 1917 were soon to eclipse its reputation for horror and catastrophe. As time went on, although men continued to fight and die here from shell fire, trench raids and occasional skirmishes, Loos became known as a "quiet sector".

Private Henry Dadd was no doubt happy enough to be transferred here after fighting in the great Somme offensives of 1916. Before the war, he had run his own rag-and-bone business in Deptford, south London. Normally a quiet man, he had a temper which, once unleashed, could be fierce. One Saturday night in 1915, an argument in a pub turned into a fight. Henry hit another man on the head with an iron bar and, next morning, he found himself in court charged with a serious offence. The magistrate found him guilty as charged and Henry was given two choices. Either he could go to prison, or he could join the army. Henry chose to enlist and, at the age of 32, he found himself in the 9th Reserve Battalion of the East Kent Regiment, "The Buffs".

Henry's unit spent time camped in Ploegsteert Woods, from where he could see the shattered ruins of Messines' church up on the ridge and he could view the fields where the Christmas truce had already become a distant memory. His fighting qualities were put to the test in the battle for Guillemont, one of the many modest rural villages that assumed huge strategic importance on the vast Somme battlefield. The fighting was bitter and it was said *"The dead lay as a thick carpet on the battleground."*[5] Now, in the cold winter of 1916–17 Henry was to be tested again on the bleak, windswept fields around Loos.

Private Dadd was chosen for a night raid on the German trenches. These were usually small-scale efforts involving a handful of soldiers who were given orders to snatch a prisoner or two for interrogation, or eliminate a troublesome enemy observation post. Sometimes, it was just to "maintain the offensive spirit" as required by higher command. The motive on this occasion was retaliation for an earlier German raid that had captured some of Henry's colleagues.

Henry and his comrades prepared to creep out through the barbed wire in front of their own trenches, crawl across No Man's Land to reach and penetrate the wire defences in front of the German positions. It was bitterly cold and snow covered the ground. Henry was issued with a white smock to cover his khaki uniform which gave him some camouflage protection.

The barbed wire entanglements were wide and Henry was still making his way on hands and knees through the British outer defences when a shell burst nearby. Pieces of metal shrapnel travelling at great speed struck Henry on the head, knocking him unconscious. When dawn came, his friends could see him lying on the wire, silent and motionless. They had no idea if he was alive or dead. It was too dangerous to go to his aid, so Henry lay there on the wire, a brown and white figure amongst the snow and the mud. The family say he was there for some days and nights, two or three, they are not sure, before he stirred and his comrades crept out to rescue him.

It is a mystery how Henry did not die either from his head wound, or a lack of water or from the extreme cold. However, medical research is beginning to understand how extremely cold temperatures shut down the body's systems and increase the chances of survival long after the brain should be clinically dead. There are well documented cases of people who have died in very cold conditions being revived many hours later.[6] One wonders where Henry's mind and soul went during that long ordeal but the family story does not tell us. When doctors finally examined him, they found Henry was suffering from pneumonia and had fragments of metal embedded in his skull. Fortunately, the surgeon was able to remove the shrapnel and Henry was sent off to recover in hospital.

During his time away from the Front, Henry decided to progress his military career. He earned a pay rise by training as a Lewis gunner and used these skills fighting with the West Yorks during the German's 1918 offensive at the Battle of the Lys. Henry Dadd survived the war, and moved to the Kent fishing town of Deal. There he resumed his trade as a rag-and-bone man and raised a family of four boys, Henry (Harry), Fred, George and John. When his grandson, Gordon, once asked him what he he'd done in the war, Henry's only response was: "I lost some good friends and I killed a lot of men." It is because of Henry Dadd that we were now walking the Loos battlefield. His great grandson, Chris Morgan, was inspired to research the War his great-grandfather had served in. Chris, in turn, had nurtured my own interest and guided me around the battlefields. The blue IGN walking map of the Loos area we were now using was the one upon which Chris had sketched the trench lines that Henry himself would have known.

Henry died in 1963 at the age of 79. A few months before he died, Henry contracted pneumonia. His grandson, Gordon, remembers as a boy hearing his grandfather shouting from his bedroom on the top floor of the family home. Gordon called to his father, Harry, and together they went up to see what was happening. They found Henry leaning out of the window, tense and angry, his mind clearly in another time and another place. Henry was holding an empty glass Lucozade bottle like a club, ready to use it against an on-coming foe. When the two of them entered the room, Henry shouted *"Harry, get Gordon out of here while I hold them off!"* Henry Dadd is buried in Deal cemetery. Somewhere, amongst the possessions of Henry's extended family are the pieces of shrapnel that the doctors gave him after they'd removed them from his head.

✷ ✷ ✷

1. *My Boy Jack* by Tonie and Valmai Holt, published by Pen and Sword Military Books 2014, page 91. All quotes reprinted with the kind permission of the publishers.

2. *Ibid* page 95.
3. *Ibid* page 121.
4. *Ibid* page 205 onwards for the case against the grave being that of Jack Kipling.
5. Barry Cuttall *148 days on the Somme* (GMS Enterprises 2000) p153, quoted in *A Parish in Wartime – St Anselm's Church, Tooting Bec* by Nick Dunne and John Pontifex www.stanselmstbec.org.uk
6. For example, one morning an ambulance crew were called out to a forest in Japan. A woman had been found dead after an overdose. The night had been cold, and she had been dead for so long that her body temperature had dropped from the normal 98.6 degrees F to around 68 degrees F. She was however successfully revived and some 20 days later left the hospital with almost no brain damage at all. See Dr Sam Parnia's *The Lazarus Effect*, published by Rider Books, 2013, pages 276–77.

The Double Crassier and Dud Corner Cemetery, Loos.
"It had the square solid character of a frontier fort."

CHAPTER NINE

The Vastness of St Vaast

Givenchy-en-Gohelle, Vimy Ridge, Arras

Up early the next morning, I managed to decode a bus timetable and spot the only bus that would take us through the suburbs towards our route for the day. Skipping breakfast, we just had time to join school children and commuters on the number 35 as it took us south towards Avion.

We got off at the last of the houses, beyond which were fields and a coal slag heap now covered in mature trees. It was a pleasant landscape, though our path beside a busy, narrow road was not enjoyable. The verge petered out in places, leaving little room on the bends for us, our packs and the approaching cars. We were aiming for the village of Givenchy-en-Gohelle and an unusual white landmark we could see on top of the high, forest covered ridge ahead. The early morning sun caught the structure perfectly, illuminating two tall, slim, vertical wings rising either side of a group of stone figures gathered at their base. Its whiteness shone brilliantly in the sun, giving it an other-worldly quality, as if an Assyrian temple had been built amidst the forests. This was the magnificent Canadian memorial to its fallen of the Great War and the crest of land rising up from the road ahead of us was Vimy Ridge.

Whilst the British were attacking Loos in 1915, the French had attacked Vimy Ridge with little success and at huge cost. Therefore, when Canadian units captured this heavily fortified German position in April 1917, their victory was celebrated as a remarkable achievement. It was the first time that the Canadian units had fought together and the battle forged a distinctly Canadian consciousness amongst the soldiers, most of whom still considered themselves to be British or Irish. Vimy Ridge is therefore as much a symbol of Canadian identity as it is the site of the great opening battle of the 1917 spring offensive. At the foot of the ridge, Givenchy village benefits from the crowds of visitors who come to pay their respects. As we walked through its quiet streets, we could see its prosperity in the freshly laid square around the church, the new primary school building and its two cafes preparing for the day ahead.

To our delight, we spotted a scallop shell waymark on a post telling us we were on the GR127 footpath that would, ultimately, lead us to the Camino and the way to Santiago de Compostela. This pilgrim path took us up the side of the ridge, through woods and then to open fields where sheep grazed behind wire fences. These were not like normal fields. For the first time on this journey, we were crossing the war's distinctive, scooped and rounded landscape where shell holes, now a century old, still pockmarked the ground. Sheep contentedly nibbled at rich, green grass covering soil that had been churned into waves and troughs once fluid, now fixed, untouched by levelling plough. Above us, the great white monument loomed large and we could see groups of tiny people gathered around its giant figures. Soon we would be amongst them but, for these moments, we were alone on this path, in this lost sea of war, watched by mildly curious sheep.

Private Will R. Bird of the 42nd Battalion, the Black Watch of Canada walked through this battlefield at dusk one evening soon after the Ridge had been taken.

"The Canadian attack of April 9 and 10 had left it a jungle of old wire and powdered brick, muddy burrows and remnants of trenches… we sat in a crater to rest… To one side of us, in a sort of alcove to the crater, three dead men were reclining, gazing incuriously before them, their faces almost black. We rose at once and climbed from the place, and almost fell over another dead man crouched in a shell hole, rifle still at hand, as if ready to spring."

Here, death was part of the landscape, the border between this life and the next particularly thin. On another night, returning late to Vimy village, Bird took shelter with two other soldiers in a shallow dug out in the side of a railway embankment.

"We snuggled in, and with a ground sheet pegged to hold over our heads we were really comfortable. In seconds I was dead to the world."

Private Bird was fast asleep when

"the ground sheet... was pulled free and fell on my face, rousing me. Then a firm warm hand seized one of mine and pulled me up to a sitting position. It was very early, as first sunshine was glittering on the dew-wet grass. I was annoyed that I should have to do some chore after being out so late. I tried to pull free. But the grip held, and as I came to a sitting position my other hand was seized and I had a look at my visitor... I was face to face with my brother Steve who had been killed in 1915!... Steve grinned as he released my hands, then put his warm hand over my mouth as I started to shout my happiness. He pointed to the sleepers in the bivvy and to my rifle and equipment. "Get your gear," he said softly. As I grabbed it, he turned and started walking away rapidly. It was hard to keep up with him... Then I noticed he had a soft cap on and no gas mask or equipment... how in the world did he know where I was sleeping? We left the company area and headed directly into a collection of ruins that had been Petit Vimy."

In the ruins, Will Bird lost sight of his brother and settled down to wait for him, dozing in the sun.

"Suddenly I was shaken awake."

However, it was not Steve, but two comrades from Will's unit who were very relieved to find him.

"What's all the row about?" Bird asked.

"You should know," came the reply, *"they're digging around that bivvy you were in. All they've found is Jim's helmet and one of Bob's legs. A big shell landed in that bivvy. They've been trying to find something of you."*

Will Bird was sure that his brother had come back from the dead that night to save him.

"I had seen Steve... His warm hands had pulled me from the bivvy. His voice had been perfectly natural. He had the old half-grin I knew so well. He had saved my life. I had joined the Methodist Church when I was fourteen and had been as decent as the average...But now I knew beyond all argument or theory, by any man learned or otherwise, that there was a hereafter, and there would never again be the slightest doubt in my mind about it." [1]

* * *

There is a danger that Vimy Ridge, with its reconstructed stone trenches and its crowds of school parties, could become a Great War theme park. However, the view from the memorial is enough to inspire genuine awe and wonder in any visitor who pauses long enough from group chatter and selfie-photos to take it all in. The memorial's huge, voluptuous statues of shrouded or virtually naked men and women were designed to represent the highest human values and the deepest human pain. They mark the summit of the ridge beyond which the land falls sharply down to the Lens–Douai plain and reveals the entire battleground of this sector of the Front. To the left, there is the Double Crassier commanding the gateway to Lens. Ahead, several conical slag heaps are scattered like dormant volcanos across a flat landscape that stretches east as far as the horizon. The world is laid out before you. To control this ridge, it seems, was to control the war.

It was late morning and we'd expected that Vimy's theme-park qualities would provide a café. We were disappointed. The village of Neuville-Saint-Vaast, we were told, was our best chance of a bakery and so we descended through shaded woods down the gentle incline of the ridge's western slope onto the D55. The bakery was indeed open and we rested near a French war memorial in the village square before continuing southwards along the D49E. A road side history panel told us that this had been a heavily fortified sector known as the Labrynthe, the scene of bitter fighting in the French attacks of 1915. Nearby, in a glade of trees, we came to a lonely memorial for 18-year-old cadet officer Augustin Leuregans. This young man had been in command of a unit of reservists, all of whom were over the age of 40. On May 30, 1915, they were pinned down in an underground bunker when they were ordered to attack the Labrynthe. The old soldiers were reluctant to leave their protective shelter but, the story goes, young Leuregans roused them with the words *"Come, my old dads, you're not going to let your child die alone."* Sure enough, Leuregans was killed almost as soon as he left the shelter, but his "old dads" did follow him and enough survived to tell the tale.

We were grateful to leave our road walking and follow a well-marked track off the D60 south through fields, along Les Quinze au Chemin d'Arras. A huge pile of sugar beet marked the end of the path and the beginning of the busy roads surrounding the suburbs of Sainte Catherine and St Nicolas. Ahead, the town of Arras unfolded before us, the massive bulk of its cathedral distorted by huge white panels of plastic protecting scaffolding and renovation work at its upper levels.

We entered the Place de Héros, one of the main squares of Arras, just after 4pm but our bed and breakfast at the Maison de Joséphine was closed. Fiona settled at a café whilst I went to claim our pilgrim stamp.

The Cathedral of Saint-Vaast, is, as its name suggests, vast. Building began in 1755, but construction was interrupted by the French Revolution and not completed until 1834. It reminded me of St Paul's Cathedral in London, with its white stone, high ceilings and wide-open spaces. Unlike

St Paul's, there were only a handful of visitors and it seemed to me a hollow, empty place. I found a little gift shop with a map of Western Europe on its wall charting the great pilgrim routes to Santiago de Compostela and to Rome. These historic ways converged as they passed through Arras and the map celebrated Saint-Vaast's witness to centuries of pilgrimage. An elderly man happily stamped our passports, but confirmed there was no Mass at the Cathedral that evening.

A collection of elaborately designed small wooden chests – reliquaries – were perched on a ledge. One appeared to contain the bones of St Vaast himself. This dark age cleric lived between AD 453 and 540 and earned his place in history for the part he played in the conversion of Clovis, the great king of the Franks. The story goes that, while returning from his victory over the Alemanni, Clovis was on his way to Rheims to be baptised when he stopped at the town of Toul, where Vaast, or Vedast as he is also known, lived. Clovis requested that a priest travel with him to instruct him on the way and Vaast was assigned to accompany the king.

Tradition tells that while on the road to Reims, they encountered a blind beggar at the bridge over the river Aisne. The man asked Vaast to help him and, when the priest blessed him, the beggar immediately recovered his sight. The miracle convinced the king of the wisdom of his decision to adopt his wife's Catholic religion and be baptised.

This was significant, as Clovis was the first king to unite the Frankish tribes. His conversion to Catholicism ensured that it would flourish in this part of Europe at a time when other Germanic tribes had adopted an alternative understanding of Christianity known as Arianism. Clovis not only laid the foundations of the modern French nation, but also the religious and political alliances that would eventually lead to the birth of the Holy Roman Empire 400 years later.

Vaast was installed as the first bishop of Arras in 499. Other miracles were attributed to him in his lifetime. On the night that he died it is said that local people saw a luminous cloud ascend from his house carrying Vaast's soul away.

St Vaast's bones would once have been the focus of pilgrimage, but not now. There were no candles lit, nor encouragements to pray at this spot. Indeed, it was hard to find the building's sacred focus. The high altar was almost in the middle with the chancel curving far behind it as deep as the nave in front. I had entered the cathedral through the small side door at the end of the chancel and the first thing to catch my eye was the gilded Great Organ high in the west end of the Nave. A notice proclaimed the quality of this instrument which boasted 74 stops and announced the dates when its next performances were to be given. Indeed, the building seemed better suited to the purposes of a concert hall than of a place of meditation, but maybe I was just seeing it through tired eyes after a long day's walking. I wanted to connect with this sacred place but felt alienated by its pomp.

Later, I read from an information leaflet that more than three quarters of the Cathedral had been destroyed in the First World War and that it had been bombed again in the Second. Despite its grandeur, I realised that the place had experienced its times of humility and maybe, knowing this, I might feel differently on a second visit. However, on this day, I had not been drawn to sit and say a prayer in the Cathedral of Saint-Vaast. Indeed, I did not even pause long enough to light a candle.

We'd grown anxious about Maison de Joséphine ever opening so it was with relief that, when we tried the doorbell again, we were welcomed inside. What a delightful place it was! We were shown into a living room that had been restored in 1930s style, invited to sit down and offered tea. The frustrations of the day left us and we accepted that the delay had been our responsibility for not using a mobile phone to confirm our arrival time.

Fiona was not hungry, so I set out alone to find an evening meal in the square. I remembered a chance encounter several years before when Chris Morgan and I had chatted in a café with a retired English couple who were walking the Via Francigena. At that time, I had barely heard of the route and my interest was sparked. It was a memorable evening, with the magic of strangers' stories shared to inspire and encourage each other. No names were exchanged but I half hoped to meet them again if I could find the same café. Alas, on this Friday night, all cafés seemed full and loud and I found it hard to choose a suitable place to eat.

I settled on one behind the town hall that could squeeze me onto a single table. It was a homely little restaurant with red and white check table cloths where people came for a night out to enjoy the house speciality, duck. Around me, the smartly dressed diners were in good spirits. I felt rather shabby in my walking trousers as I sat writing my notes of the day's walk and waiting for my steak to arrive. As I did so, I became aware of a firearm placed on the radiator beside me. It was a rifle of 1914 vintage, lying there as if forgotten by a soldier who'd been hurriedly called away.

* * *

1. *Ghosts Have Warm Hands* by Will R. Bird MM, pages 25–29. First published 1968, republished 2002 by CEF Books, Ontario, Canada and quoted with their kind permission. Will Bird survived the war and became a successful writer.

*"From the summit of Vimy Ridge the land falls sharply down
to the Lens–Douai plain revealing the entire battleground"*

CHAPTER TEN

Shortcut to Albert

Arras, Albert, Mailly-Maillet, Courcelle-au-Bois

Our day's walking to Arras had been more draining than we'd expected and we realised that the next day's journey was too long to walk as planned. Our pilgrimage was not meant to be an ordeal, so we decided to trim a few kilometres off by taking the train to Albert. From there we could walk back into the countryside to the farm house in the small village of Courcelle-au-Bois where we'd booked our accommodation. This was not on the official Via Francigena route, which carried on from Arras further to the east to Bapaume, but the detour seemed essential for this section of the pilgrimage.

Albert was a key front line town during the First World War. Here the French had succeeded in holding the German advance in 1914 and its railway link became key to supplying British endeavours on the Somme battlefields of 1916. Thousands of French, British, Empire and, in 1918, German troops passed through Albert during those years of war and, for that reason alone, this is a place of pilgrimage. However, Albert had been attracting pilgrims for centuries before the war gave its gruesome blessing and kings and saints were among those drawn by devotion to a statue of the Madonna that was found buried in a sheep field nearby.[1]

According to tradition, sometime in the 11th century a shepherd was grazing his flock in fields near the Ancre river. He noticed that one of his ewes had left the others to graze at a particular spot so he called to it. When it refused to move, he went over, striking the ground with his staff. "Stop, shepherd," a voice called out, "you are hurting me!" The shepherd pulled his staff from the soil and to his surprise found it stained with blood. Digging down into the earth, he found a statue of the Virgin whose forehead was marked with the blow from his staff.

A chapel was built and over the centuries pilgrims who sought healing came to Notre-Dame de Brebières (Our Lady of the Ewes). Today, a modest stone memorial beside a narrow lane on the outskirts of Albert marks the place where tradition says the shepherd discovered the statue. In the centre of town, the old church was replaced in 1909 by a magnificent neo-Byzantine, red brick basilica crowned with a bell-tower 250 feet tall. At its top was The Golden Virgin, a spectacular bronze image of the Madonna holding her baby Jesus up to the heavens.

Tragically, war came just five years later and the basilica was badly damaged by shell fire. Early in the conflict, the tower took a glancing blow which caused the statue of Our Lady and Child to tilt over by 90 degrees. As a result, instead of offering her son to God on high, she seemed to be offering Him to the anxious and battle-weary soldiers who marched through the street below. A Canadian clergyman, Canon Frederick Scott, wrote in his memoirs that, in Albert

"every building had either been shattered or damaged by shells. From the spire of the cathedral hung at right angles the beautiful bronze image of the Blessed Virgin, holding up her child above her head for the adoration of the world. It seemed to me as if there were something appropriate in the strange position the statue now occupied, for, as the battalions marched past the church, it looked as if they were receiving a parting benediction from the Infant Saviour." [2]

The statue held its haunting pose for most of the war. The Madonna and her child seemed to be charmed, surviving subsequent shellfire without further damage. The story grew that whoever made her fall would lose the war and her presence became a good luck charm for the Allied cause. When, in March 1918, Albert fell to the rapid German advance, the British were not sentimental. Concerned that the remains of the basilica's tower offered too good an observation point for the occupying German forces, they trained their own guns on Our Lady and brought her and her Son crashing to the ground.

After the war, the basilica was rebuilt as close as possible to its original design. The 15ᵗʰ century statue of Notre Dame de Brebières was returned to her place above the high altar, and a new bronze statue was erected on the pinnacle of the great tower's dome. Of all the churches I have visited in France, this is one of my favourites. Its red brick construction and Byzantine mosaics recall the richness of London's Catholic Cathedral at Westminster. There is grandeur, but humility too in its simplicity and the warmth of its colours. The basilica is always open and candles burn at its altars. During one visit, Chris Morgan and I sat spellbound in its quietness as a small boy, no more than five years of age, left his mother to climb the steps behind the high altar and sing an *Ave Maria* at the foot of Our Lady's statue. The purity of the little lad's voice and the joy in his face as he returned to his proud mother touched our souls.

* * *

As the train from Arras pulled into Albert railway station we could see the great basilica with its high brick tower rising to the sky. The sun was hot and, from the top of the tower, the bronze image of the Madonna holding her baby Jesus up to the heavens shone gold in the sun's rays. Unlike Ypres, or Vimy, Albert is not overrun by visitors. Most coaches will make straight for Thiepval and the memorials on the battlefield ridge. Albert itself is a small town with a handful of hotels and a modest museum in underground tunnels which run from the basilica to a park by the Ancre river. It is prosperous enough but probably not as prosperous as its heritage deserves. When the basilica was first built in 1909, Pope Leo XIII hoped it would make Albert "the Lourdes of the North of France." Although there haven't been any recent miracles or apparitions, its memories of the Great War confirm it as a sacred place deserving of many more pilgrims.

The path took us north from the railway station into the hills and villages of the reserve areas that served the great battles of 1916. Their small cemeteries are rarely visited by students of the Great War. The sun boiled down on us as we worked our way northwards along tracks and minor roads towards Martinsart and Englebelmer. At Mailly-Maillet, we paused to study the spectacular late Gothic sculptures on the porch of the 16th Century church of St Peter. At their centre, Jesus sat looking down on us, His wrists bound in rope, a prisoner waiting for His execution. Opposite the church, behind a long brick wall enclosing the grounds of a chateau, another prisoner, a British soldier, had once spent his last night, awaiting his execution.

Private James Crozier had enlisted in the Royal Irish Guards in 1914. His mother, Elizabeth, had gone with him to the West Belfast recruiting office, pleading with him all the while to change his mind. The recruiting officer, who by coincidence, was also named Crozier, remembered the boy when he came to write his memoirs and gave him the pseudonym "Crocker". Major Frank Crozier recalled that the boy's mother had threatened to tell the soldiers that James was only 17, but she was still unable to change her son's mind. Major Crozier kindly reassured Elizabeth that he would look after her son and James duly enlisted.

It was another year before James, whose age was by then officially recorded as 19, arrived in France. Frank Crozier had been promoted to Lieutenant Colonel and, during that bitter winter, was sharing the danger and misery of his troops on the front line.

On January 31, 1916 young James Crozier had had enough. He went missing and was picked up 25 miles away, far behind the lines. He was returned to his unit and court-martialled. The penalty for desertion was death but, before passing sentence, the court first sought the recommendations of his commanding officer, Frank Crozier. Despite what he'd said to the boy's mother, Lieutenant Colonel Crozier decided that military discipline had to be upheld. He offered no evidence that might persuade the court to commute the sentence.

James Crozier spent his last night drinking the rum and whisky his commanding officer had provided for him. By the time the Military Police came to take him to the place of execution, James was unconscious and it was with difficulty that he was tied to a post in the garden of the chateau at Mailly-Maillet. Opposite him, a firing party from his own battalion made their final preparations. On the other side of the wall the rest of the battalion were paraded on the street where Lieutenant Colonel Frank Crozier was in command of proceedings.

Standing on a mound, Frank Crozier could see over the wall to the execution site. When the officer in charge of the firing party raised his white handkerchief the Lieutenant Colonel called the battalion to attention. When the handkerchief fell, the executioners fired. The officer in charge checked his prisoner but found that James Crozier was wounded, not dead. Despite only being a few yards from their victim, several soldiers had no stomach for the task and shot wide. It fell to the officer in charge of the firing party to administer the final, fatal shot.

Perhaps remembering their conversation in the Belfast recruiting office, Lieutenant Colonel Crozier tried to protect James' grieving mother and attempted to record the death as a battlefield casualty. As he explained to the padre

> *"War is all pot-luck, some get a hero's halo, others a coward's cross. But this man volunteered in '14. His heart was in the right place then, even if his feet are cold in '16."*[3]

Unfortunately, the Lieutenant Colonel was not successful and Elizabeth Crozier was neither spared the truth of her son's death, nor did she qualify for the financial allowances normally given to the relatives of soldiers killed in action.

Our sympathies automatically go to the young man who, it seems, cracked under the terrible conditions in which he had to serve. However, we must be more cautious in automatically casting his commanding officer as the villain in this sad story. Despite his words of assurance at the recruiting office, Frank Crozier had a job to do. This included maintaining the military discipline upon which the collective endeavour relied. Managing desertion, in all its forms, was a real concern for the authorities. Researchers Corns and Hughes-Wilson estimate that there were around 1,000 desertions a month amongst the BEF in 1916. However, executions were, in fact, rare. Only 306 men died in this way throughout the whole war.[4] It appears that Frank Crozier showed compassion where he could, within an overall view that James was indeed guilty as charged and had no grounds to have his sentence commuted. A hundred years later, it is tempting to judge the men involved, yet who can say how, in the circumstances and within the values of the time, we would have acted either in the Private's shoes, or the Lieutenant Colonel's? Once the macabre logic of war is engaged and death no longer has its peacetime value, the framework within which decisions are made changes and good people do terrible things.

In this one story there is all the desperate sadness of the time. As we left Mailly-Maillet, I pondered the timelessness of that image of Christ the bound prisoner and regretted that I could not pause longer to look in the village for James Crozier's grave.

* * *

1. Saint King Louis IX in the 13th century, S Collette de Corbie in the 14th/15th Century, King Jean II (Jean le Bon), 14th Century, St Vincent de Paul, 17th Century, and St Benoît Labre, 18th Century all came on pilgrimage to Albert. The author Henry Williamson, most famous for his book *Tarka the Otter*, served in Albert. His autobiographical book, *The Golden Virgin* took its title from the statue on top of the tower of Albert's basilica.
2. *The Great War as I Saw It* by Canon Frederick G. Scott CMG, DSO, pages 92, 93, first published in 1922, reprinted 2000 by CEF Books, Ontario, Canada and quoted with the publisher's kind permission.
3. *A Brass Hat in No-Man's Land* by Frank Crozier (Cape, 1930) https://archive.org/details/brasshatinnomans00fran/page/82/mode/2up Frank

Crozier attained the rank of Brigadier General and his involvement in the case of James Crozier is discussed in *Blindfold and Alone* by Cathryn Corns and John Hughes-Wilson (Cassell 2001, republished by Orion Publishing Co, 2005) pages 305–307. See also *Shot at Dawn* by Julian Putkowski and Julian Sykes (Pen and Sword, 1989) and William Moore's *The Thin Yellow Line* (Wordsworth Military Library 1974).

4. *Blindfold and Alone*, Corns and Hughes –Wilson, page 447.

*"At Mailly-Maillet, Jesus sat looking down on us,
his wrists bound in rope, a prisoner waiting for his execution"*

CHAPTER ELEVEN

In Search of Albert Bassett

Courcelles-au-Bois, Thiepval, Albert

A farm track took us to the edge of Courcelles-au-Bois and L'Amartinierre farmhouse where we were booked for the night. We rang the iron bell that hung by the great wooden gate but, as expected, there was no reply. Our hostess, Christine, and her family were at a friend's 50th birthday party so she'd left the key to our room in a safe place for us to collect. The 14 or so kilometres from Albert in the boiling sun had exhausted me and I was content to sit on a bench in the farm yard whilst Fiona boiled a kettle in the kitchen. We were the only guests and we had all of the comfortable visitors' annex to ourselves.

Courcelles-au-Bois was a small village of 84 inhabitants where nothing seemed to be happening. The village church stood on a little mound and appeared to be derelict, its windows covered by huge metal plates. There were no shops, cafes or bars. For our evening meal, we'd brought some bread, cheese and ham from Arras and we made do with multiple infusions of our last peppermint teabag.

When we'd eaten, I went out for one more exploration of the village. This time, I noticed that the door to the church was open. Inside, a couple of women were busy dusting and sweeping. "We are getting ready for Mass tomorrow," one said, "come and join us." I studied a faded schedule pinned to the church door that charted Sunday Masses in the surrounding villages. The dates covered the period from September 2014 to February 2015. Courcelles-au-Bois appeared only once, with October 19, time 9.30 am proudly highlighted in yellow.

Next morning, Christine brought chunks of delicious homemade bread for our breakfast. She spoke excellent English and was delighted when we said we were planning to go to church. "You will be very welcome. I will be there too. I was married in that church and today is a very special day. It is the only Mass that will be said there this year."

It was another beautiful morning and the church, so long empty, was alive with people and chatter. Christine was among those greeting arrivals at the door and she introduced us to a small, wiry man in his 70s dressed in open-necked shirt and casual trousers. He welcomed us enthusiastically. "*Les marchers,*" he said as he shook our hands. This was our priest, Fr Joël Dulin.

The metal panels were still over the windows but I could now see that their design included lots of small holes to allow plenty of sunlight into the church. The stained-glass images of Christ and the saints were beautifully illuminated and fresh cut flowers decorated the altar. All the work that had gone into cleaning and dusting this little church had been worth it. The whole place seemed to glow with love and care.

There were nearly 50 people in the congregation. The vast majority were older women, but there were several men and one family with three young children. Fr Joël appeared from behind the altar, now dressed in a full length white alb with a bright multicoloured stole draped like a scarf over his shoulders. He called us to order and, with a clear and tuneful voice, led us in an opening hymn. The congregation responded in kind. There were no instruments to accompany us and our music was all the better for it. We knew our voices alone could celebrate this day and we rose to the occasion. Not a voice was out of tune. Although Fiona and I did not understand a word of detail, Fr Joël's natural warmth and enthusiasm said enough. He had a rapport with those present and everyone was delighted to be here, celebrating this little church which for many, like Christine, held very special memories. We felt honoured to be part of it.

All too soon, the Mass was over. Wearing his casual clothes once more, Fr Joël strode quickly down the aisle waving to everyone as he left. He had another Mass to get to this morning. Hooked over his shoulder was a multicoloured fabric bag containing his notes and books. The word "Ecuador" was woven into it. Christine told us later that Fr Joël had worked for many years in the overseas missions and still travelled back to Ecuador regularly. It was relevant preparation for his role now as a travelling priest who covered long distances to say Mass in scattered parishes. Once a missionary to the people of Ecuador, he was now a missionary to his own people of France.

The occasion was over and the community began to disperse. Christine had kindly agreed to take our heavy bags into Albert and leave them at the Ibis where we would stay for the next two nights. She was busy now with her friends and with family plans, so we quickly said our thanks and "goodbyes" and prepared to set off on our morning's walk. However, before we left the village there was one more story we needed to explore.

On May 20, 1940, a German tank had rolled into the main square at Albert. The speed of the Germans' advance had caught the British units in the town completely by surprise. Within hours, the fighting was over and the Nazi occupation of this part of France had begun.[1]

Four years later, the D Day landings in June 1944 had encouraged local people to fight back against the occupiers. On September 1st, German soldiers came to Courcelles-au-Bois searching for a member of the resistance they believed was involved in an attack. They were so certain he was in the village that they took a group of residents and lined them up near the cross roads. The order went out: *"Unless Louis Thomas comes out and surrenders, the hostages will be shot, one at a time."*

Louis Thomas was, indeed, in the village. He was hiding in a farm building and, from an upper window overlooking the street, he could see what the soldiers were doing. To prevent the hostages' execution, he left his hiding place and began running up the road leading away from the village. He was in full view of the troops and, as he approached the wayside cross by the cemetery, they opened fire.

Christine had told us that the farm building where Louis Thomas had hidden was still there. We walked past its red brick wall and saw the upper window from which he had assessed the situation and made his plan. He could have chosen another way out of the farm, into the fields and hedgerows, where he might have had a chance of escape. But he knew that others would pay the price and he couldn't accept that. Louis Thomas died within yards of the farm building and the place on the road where he fell is now marked by a simple white memorial stone, a tribute to his bravery. With his sacrifice, the soldiers kept their word and released their hostages, unharmed.

* * *

The Battle of the Somme began on July 1, 1916. The British forces had expected the seven days of artillery bombardment beforehand to obliterate the German defences and make it easy for the advancing infantry to capture their positions. Terrifying as it was, the shell fire was not enough to cut the barbed wire entanglements nor penetrate the deep shelters where the German soldiers waited. As a result, when the first attacking troops left their trenches at 7.30 am, they were met by machine gun and rifle fire across the entire length of the 18-mile front. On July 1, the British army suffered its highest ever casualty rate in a single day. By sunset, an estimated 57,470 were killed, wounded or missing.

July 1, 1916 was a beautiful, sunny day. So was this, the fifth day of our pilgrimage from Fromelles. In such conditions, there is nowhere more exhilarating to walk. The hills open up around you. Gentle climbs along tracks through fields of crops are rewarded with spectacular views and huge open panoramas. There is a great sense of space. The sky is a vast, blue dome encompassing landmarks of unimaginable human endeavour, suffering and endurance. Cemeteries and memorials are scattered across the hilltops and the valleys. Woods destroyed by bombardments a hundred years ago have reclaimed their original patterns; villages, rebuilt to their pre-war specifications, now have their place in history as well as in the landscape. As you become familiar with each one, you can see how they connect to each other and reform the battle lines of July 1916.

Our path took us along a straight, muddy track leading from a farm towards the front lines. It was a picturesque route, with sunbeams flickering through mature trees either side of the path. As we approached the end, we noticed some people walking through the field to our right, calling out to each other. Ahead, two men stood on the path watching them. Each had a shotgun over his arm. The first one looked at us and told us, in French, that this was a private road. We apologised profusely and then indicated the little war cemetery we could see beyond them. This seemed to give some legitimacy to our presence. When one of the beaters called to him from the field, he shouted back to reassure him: *"Les Anglais sont perdus," "the English are lost"*, before nodding us on our way.

The gate at the end of the track did, indeed, say *"Privée"* and black and yellow incident tape stretched across it emphasised the instruction not to cross this line. We hadn't seen any such sign at the other end, but then few visitors would approach the cemetery from this direction. Most would be travelling along the main road.

Sucrerie Cemetery took its name from the sugar factory nearby and a peaceful glade of trees now sheltered the 1,100 men buried here. A fresh red paper poppy wreath marked one of them and I went over to read the dedication. When I saw the name on the tombstone, I realised that I knew this soldier's story.

After the war, the body of Rifleman James Crozier was brought to Sucrerie Cemetery from Mailly-Maillet. In 2006, 90 years after his death on February 27, 1916, James Crozier was pardoned together with all the 306 men who had been executed for desertion. The document signed by the Secretary of State for Defence, Des Browne, stated that the pardon *"stands as recognition that he was one of many victims of the First World War and that execution was not a fate he deserved."*[2]

* * *

Leaving the cemetery, we were soon standing on the line of the British forward trenches of 1916. These next three miles are probably the best-known section of the battlefield, not least because of the film taken on July 1st by Geoffrey Malins, the Army's official photographer. Yellow and black tape again blocked our path along "the sunken road", a deep cutting between fields lined with hedgerows where Malins had filmed troops waiting to launch their attack on the village of Beaumont Hamel. Armed hunters now stood casually at the place where soldiers had once gathered anxiously awaiting their fate.

Taking another path, we reached the huge Hawthorn Crater created by a mine detonated under the German trenches at the start of the battle. Malins filmed the explosion from the British lines just a couple of hundred yards away and captured one of the most memorable moving images of the Great War. From there we climbed the hill from Beaumont Hamel to Newfoundland Park, another place of terrible carnage on July 1st. Here, as at Vimy Ridge, the battlefield and its trenches have been preserved as a memorial to the Canadian soldiers who died here in such huge numbers. Our road ran on past the entrance and down towards the Ancre valley. Looking over to our left, to open fields just past the woods in Newfoundland Park, our thoughts turned to Fiona's grandfather, Albert Morgan Bassett, who had served in this area with the 6th Battalion of the Cheshire regiment.

Albert did not leave a personal record of his war-time experiences. The family only knew that he had been gassed at some stage during his service. However, a battalion has, at most, a thousand or so officers and men and so Albert would have known, and been known by, many of those referred to in the official records. These reports are, therefore, a good guide to what Private Albert Bassett would have seen, and heard and been a part of.[3]

We were now walking along the same roads that Albert had marched during the final stages of the Battle of the Somme. Crossing the Ancre river, Mill Road began to climb steeply out of the river valley. Here we were following the line of No Man's Land on July 1, 1916. The land that now sloped down to our right, to the edge of Thiepval Wood, was where the British forces waited to attack. To our left, the land rose up the hillside to the German lines just a few yards away. A modern monument, the Ulster Tower, now stands tall where the German front line once was. About half a kilometre beyond it, on the highest point of the ridge, was where a huge network of fortifications, the Schwaben Redoubt, had withstood the British assault for months. It wasn't until the end of October 1916 that the Redoubt was finally captured after terrible fighting.

From the Ulster Tower, it is just a kilometre or so to the village of Thiepval. By the time Albert's 6th Battalion arrived in late August 1916, artillery had pounded the village and its chateau into rubble, but German strongpoints, like the Schwaben Redoubt, still held the all-important high ground. Private 66005 Albert Morgan Bassett was posted to trenches below where the Ulster Tower now stands, just a few hundred yards from the German lines running along the hillside above him. It was his first experience of the "front line" and it was a very dangerous place to be.

∗ ∗ ∗

Albert Bassett was only 17 when he joined the Cheshire Regiment in early 1916. Born on December 18, 1898, he lived at Dolgoch, in the North Wales village of Bethesda. He was the youngest of three children, with two brothers, Oscar who became a businessman, and Heber who became headmaster of a school in the Anfield district of Liverpool. Their father had died when Albert was just three years old.

Albert probably signed up with the Cheshires at their Territorial Unit in Rhyl, travelling to France in the Spring of 1916 with the 1/6th Battalion (the only unit of the Cheshires to serve overseas as the 2/6th and 3/6th Battalions remained in the UK). Fortunately, on July 1st, his unit were held in reserve at Bethune, far away from the killing fields. It was not until late August that they were brought into the line of the Somme battlefield.

On September 1, 1916 Lieutenant Colonel W.H. Stanway DSO MC, Commanding Officer of the 6th Battalion typed into the Battalion's War Diary:

"Battalion in trenches occupying right sector north of Thiepval. Our artillery actively engaged all day demolishing enemy wire. Enemy replied vigorously with H.E. (high explosive) damaging our fire and communications trenches badly. All available men engaged in clearing debris and making good damage done. Officers patrols went out and reconnoitred enemy wire and trenches. Captain Kirk and party of 6 OR (other ranks) entered enemy trench and finding all quiet proceeded along same. Noticing a light proceeding from a dugout when entered and along with two men he surprised three Huns in the dugout. These he immediately disposed of and was able to obtain information of considerable value in view of the forthcoming operations, afterwards returning safely with his party to our lines."

Captain Kirk was awarded the Military Cross for his work that day.

Only the officers are routinely named in War Diaries, recording their arrivals, their deeds and departures. Albert was a lowly private, an OR (other rank), one of the many unnamed, so we cannot be sure of the details of his experience. Yet the diary gives us tangible clues to build on. It is unlikely he would have been part of that raiding party, but the enemy's "vigorous" barrage of high explosives would have shaken his body and his nerves. Surprisingly, only three wounded are recorded as being taken to hospital that day, a very small number of casualties for all the H.E. raining down on them. The next day, September 2, the exchanges of artillery fire continued, but the 1/6 Cheshires were withdrawn from the front-line and replaced by Battalions from the Sussex and Hampshire Regiments for an attack the following morning when *"front line troops rushed the Boche line."* It is not clear from the diary how successful the operation was but, by 6 pm, the Cheshires were brought forward to relieve the assaulting Battalions and again take over their original positions in the front line. No deaths were recorded amongst the Cheshires, but 15 OR were wounded and taken to hospital.

September 4 is reported in the War Diary as

"Situation quiet. All available men engaged night and day repairing damage to trenches and in removing wounded and dead from No Mans Land. 3 OR to hospital wounded."

It would have been a hard day's work for Albert, digging, shoring up the trench walls, perhaps creeping out over the parapet to help bring in the injured and the dead. Was there an informal truce to allow this to happen? If so, it is not mentioned. September 5, 1916 is again recorded as *"Situation quiet."* However, Lieutenant Colonel Stanway goes on to note:

"Enemy sent over a good number of gas shells during day but without effect."

It's hard to imagine that these fearful weapons could have exploded *"without effect."* Lt Colonel Stanway does not say if it was the efficient use of gas masks, or a change in the prevailing wind that neutralised the toxic vapours. Just three OR were wounded, two being sent to hospital, with a third well enough to remain on duty. A higher number, seven OR, reported sick and were sent to hospital which suggests that the conditions in the trenches at that time presented greater hazards to health than the weapons being hurled at them. That evening, the Black Watch arrived and Albert would have been as pleased as anyone in the Battalion to be leaving the front line. The Regimental History[4] puts these incidents in the context of the wider Battle of Pozieres, which ran from July 23 to September 3. It notes: *"Our 6th Battalion was in the trenches in front of Thiepval during this period and so earned the honour for this battle which was mainly concerned with the fighting for Mouquet Farm."* Thus, Private Albert Morgan Bassett, although unnamed, finds his first place in the Regimental Battle Honours.

* * *

On leaving Thiepval, the 6th Battalion were ordered to reserve billets at Englebelmer, one of the villages Fiona and I had walked through the previous day on the way from Albert to Courcelles-au-Bois.

As the crow flies, it is about six kilometres from Thiepval to Englebelmer (which is spelt Englebeimer in the War Diary). It was comfortably far enough behind the front line for the Cheshires to expect a few days of relative peace and safety but, that night, Lieutenant Colonel Stanway records *"Enemy shelled billets with gas shells between 1 and 2am. Battalion took cover in cellars and wore gas helmets which were quite effective."* Each day, from September 6th to September 11th, the enemy shelled the village with H.E. or shrapnel whilst the Battalion *"engaged in trench fatigues"*, the routine housework of repairing trenches, building dugouts and sinking wells. It seems that the shelling was having little effect until, on September 12, it struck several houses, killing one soldier and wounding two others. That afternoon, orders came to move the battalion back to the front line but this time to the left sector at Beaumont Hamel *"occupying front and support lines, and the reserve lines at Fort Jackson and Fort Moulin."*[5] This was the area by the entrance to Newfoundland Park we had been walking through when our thoughts had first turned to Albert. The Cheshires' trenches lay in the open fields north of the hamlet of Hamel, the land sloping away from the woods around Newfoundland Park down towards the Ancre valley. The German lines were not far away.

On September 15:

"At 5am two parties consisting of one officer and 50 OR each after artillery preparation and under cover of barrage, proceeded into No Mans Land to raid the enemy trenches and to obtain identification. Owing to the fact that the trenches opposite the gaps in the enemy wire had been filled in with knife rests[6] and also the heavy hostile machine gun and rifle fire, it was found to be impossible to make an entry, and the parties were forced to return to our lines."

One officer, and fifteen OR were wounded, and one soldier was killed.

The days passed and the War Diary records the routine of shellfire, trench repairs and fatigues *"repairing and draining trenches."* The weather was *"inclement, causing numerous falls of earth in the various trenches. Fatigue parties engaged day and night clearing up and draining. Also sinking sump pits and laying trench boards."* It must have been miserable.

On September 22, the weather improved but now enemy snipers added to the risks presented by trench mortar, gas and artillery shelling. Lieutenant Colonel Stanway was untroubled, *"without effect"* is all he wrote. His mind was busy planning another raid on the enemy lines for September 26. This was to be a diversion to take the enemy's attention away from the main attack on the Thiepval Ridge across the other side of the Ancre Valley. The detailed order marked "Secret" is attached to the War Diary and gives a fascinating insight into the organisation behind even a relatively small action such as this. Specific trench map references are given for the points at which the enemy trenches were to be entered and when the map is consulted today we can see clearly where the British line bulges to bring it closer to the German front trenches at a point named "Mary Redan".[7]

At 9 pm, four officers and 75 OR in two parties

"got out safely into No Mans Land under cover of the artillery barrage and on the same lifting, an officer and a number of men rushed the enemy trenches. These were found to be full of knife rests and wire and they had considerable difficulty in extricating themselves. During this time the covering party had taken up positions on the enemy parapet and although exposed to heavy cross machine gun fire and grenades they effectively kept the enemy at bay by throwing grenades until the party in the trench has freed themselves and got out again."

It sounds like the raid was a shambles. Its purpose had been

"to capture and kill as many of the enemy as possible, to secure identification if possible, to lower the morale of the enemy"

but there is no reference in the War Diary to suggest that Lieutenant Colonel Stanway believed any of these objectives were achieved. All that appears after his account of the action are the casualties for the day:

"2 OR killed, 7 OR wounded. 5 OR wounded at duty. 9 OR to hospital sick."

However, by the time the Regimental History was written, the records were more upbeat.

"To assist the main attack on the Thiepval Ridge, on 26th (September), the 118th Brigade made a feint attack by smoke, in the area north of Hamel. Our 6th Battalion raided the enemy trenches in conjunction with this attack. Under cover of a barrage, they crossed no-man's-land at 9pm and rushed the enemy trenches. A fierce fight ensued. While the covering party on the enemy parapet kept the enemy at bay in face of heavy machine gun fire, another party attempted to clear the enemy trenches. The trenches were found to be blocked with "knife rests" and loose wire. All the German garrison were killed or driven off, and our men withdrew with some difficulty, with a loss of 12 men."[8]

We do not know what part Albert played in this operation but, as winter approached, there was one more action still to come that would take him and the whole Battalion into a full-scale attack.

What became known as The Battle of the Ancre began on November 13 and finished five days later on the 18th. The formidable Schwaben Redoubt, situated at the highest point of the ridge just north of Thiepval village, had finally been captured the month before and it was here that, on November 13:

"Our 6th Battalion (39th Division) was formed up in the Schwaben redoubt ready to advance in four lines, part of the main attack. Zero was fixed for 5-45am."[9]

The plan was to attack the hamlet of St Pierre Divion by following the German's Strasburg Line of defences that led to it from the Schwaben Redoubt and then take Mill Trench which ran from the hamlet parallel to the Ancre river. All the resources of the Battalion were fully committed to the advance and it is almost certain that Albert would have been in one of the four waves of attacking troops. However, the weather was now having a major impact on the landscape. Conditions were terrible. Water and mud were everywhere.

"To make movement at all possible, duck-board tracks were laid from Thiepval to the assembly area. The trenches had been so shot about and damaged by weather that even in daylight it was hard to locate one's position or even to say whether one was in a trench or not. Fifteen yards a minute was the fastest that could be calculated on. Evacuation of the wounded was almost impossible. Men had to sit down and pull their legs out of the mud."[10]

To add to the difficulties, there was also thick fog. Not surprisingly, the 6th Battalion lost direction in their attack and, at first, missed their main objective. However, they regained their bearings and by 8.30 am they had captured Mill Trench along the banks of the river at a cost of 167 casualties. Among them was Captain Richard Kirk who had won the Military Cross for his work leading the raid on September 1[st.] He had been killed leading B Company in the first wave of attack.

* * *

The 6th Battalion's service at the Somme ended with its assault on St Pierre Divion. Soon afterwards winter put an end to offensive action and the Battle of the Somme was officially closed. The ridge at Thiepval had been taken and today it is the focus of pilgrimage for all who visit. Fiona and I walked up the steps and through the Memorial's towering arch inscribed with 72,000 names of the Missing. Beyond, a path lined with what looked like empty flagpoles led us away from the well cared for grounds into open fields. All that remained of the fortifications that had dominated this land were a few crumbling concrete blocks in the hedgerows. As we descended towards Avuley and the town of Albert, we gave thanks that Albert Bassett's name was not amongst those inscribed on the Thiepval Memorial.

Surviving the hardships and the hazards of his time in the Somme sector, Albert and the 6th Battalion moved north to Ypres for the Battle of Passchendaele before returning to the Somme in 1918 to face the German Spring offensive when it broke through the British lines and threatened to win the war. These were desperate times but, when the attack was halted at Amiens and at Ypres, the Allies counterattacked and began to drive the exhausted German forces back through the territory they had conquered. Albert travelled north again to the Ypres sector and was in Belgium, at Fourquepire, when the Armistice brought the War to an end on November 11, 1918. However, it was not until August 1919 that he was able to leave the British camp at Etaples in France and return home. His service had earned him the right to wear the Victory Medal and the British War Medal.

Albert met his wife to be, Lily Davies, in Colwyn Bay. He was training to be a master baker, she to be a pastry cook. They married in 1925 and moved to Lily's home village of Betws-y-Coed in North Wales where their first child, Joan, was born in January 1927. Edna and Oscar followed and the family moved to Lily's mother's house, Bod Iddon, at the end of the village close to the Miners' footbridge over the River Conwy. During our family visits there we would go to sleep with the sound of the Conwy's water rushing between the rocks. On the living room wall there was a picture of Albert in his military uniform. It showed a relaxed, smiling young man who, after the war, had set up a dramatic society in the village and was fondly remembered for his sense of humour and his excellent impersonations of Charlie Chaplin.

However, Albert's wartime experiences had taken a heavy physical toll. In one of my last telephone conversations with her, Albert's eldest daughter, Joan, remembered him with affection. For the last three years of his life he was an invalid, sitting white-haired beside the fire wrapped in a blanket. Albert had difficulty swallowing and breathing so he lived on liquid food and slept in a specially built cabin in the garden where he could benefit from fresh air at night. Despite his illness, Joan remembered him always taking time to help her with her Maths homework and she credited him with helping her be top of her class at school. She had just celebrated her tenth birthday when Albert Bassett died on February 4, 1937. He was only 38 years of age. The medical certificate recorded the cause as *"multiple fibroids in the intestines"* and the family were in no doubt that his years in the trenches had been the source of his disease.

* * *

At first glance, the Ibis Hotel in Albert is not a place you would expect to become fond of. Set on the very edge of town in a modern industrial estate, it is a system-built three-storey box of a building without any obvious charm. The giant plaster statue of a British Tommy in its grounds looks as if it belongs in a Great War theme park. However, whatever shallow marketing ideas inspired the designers, they could not undermine the dignity of the position the hotel now occupies. This location, plus the friendliness of the staff and the good value of the food and accommodation, has made it the natural base for the many visits I have made to the Somme before, and after, our Via Francigena journey.

The Ibis sits at the boundary between town and country, beside the last roundabout out of town and just under the crest of the ridge of hills that marked the front line in 1916. Troops marched up the long straight road from the basilica in the centre of Albert to camp here in the relative safety of the hillside, known as Tara Hill. Protected from the angle of any falling shells they and their horses could move relatively freely on grass covered fields unscarred by combat.

Beyond the roundabout, the old Roman road continues its arrow-straight path between rows of trees towards the next major town, Bapaume. The Albert-Bapaume road divides the Somme battlefront as neatly as a geometrical axis. The battlefields unfold on either side and, from the Ibis Hotel, you can walk to them in twenty minutes. Where the hotel grounds meet the main road there is a small war cemetery, Bapaume Post. It is here that a young Canadian, Henry Scott, is buried.

Henry's father, Canon Frederick G Scott, wrote a vivid memoir of his service as a Padre in the Great War. In it he tells how he and Henry had their final meeting in Albert.

"I had the great joy, therefore, of having my second son near me for six days. His battalion, the 87th, was camped on a piece of high ground to the right of "Tara Hill", and from my window I could see the officers and men walking about in their lines. It was a great privilege..."[11]

Henry's unit were preparing to join an attack on the Germans' Regina Trench, several kilometres north east of Albert. On October 21, 1916, Henry Scott was killed in that attack and his body hastily buried in a shell hole. A few weeks later, before dawn on a cold November morning, Canon Scott set out from Albert to try and find his son. His account of that journey is remarkable.

On reaching the British front line, Canon Scott met a message runner who knew where Henry's body was buried. The soldier offered to take him there:

"We walked back along the communications trench and turned into one on the right, peering over the top every now and then to see if we could recognize anything corresponding to the marks on our map. Suddenly the runner, who was looking over the top, pointed far away to a lonely white cross that stood at a point where the ground sloped down through the mist towards Regina Trench. At once we climbed out of the trench and made our way over the slippery ground and past the

deep shell holes to where the white cross stood out in the solitude. We passed many bodies which were still unburied, and here and there were bits of accoutrement which had been lost during the advance. When we came up to the cross, I read my son's name upon it, and knew that I had reached the object I had in view."

In the chaos of battle, it had not been possible to know the exact location of Henry's body. The runner had to dig in several places around the cross before something white was revealed.

"It was my son's left hand, with his signet ring upon it. They had removed his identification disc, revolver and pocket-book, so the signet ring was the only thing which could have led to his identification. It was really quite miraculous that we should have made the discovery. The mist was lifting now, and the sun to the east was beginning to light up the ground. We heard the crack of bullets, for the Germans were sniping us. I had the runner go down into a shell hole, while I read the burial service, and then took off the ring."

Canon Scott and the runner both returned to the trench unharmed. A few days later, on November 25th, Canon Scott travelled to the small graveyard on Tara Hill, close to where Henry's unit had been encamped. Henry's body had been brought here from the battlefield and Canon Scott was once more able to pray over him as he was finally laid to rest.

After sunset I walked from the hotel to pay my respects at Bapaume Post Cemetery. In the distance, the Virgin and Child shone gold above the basilica, caught in a spotlight's beam. Overhead, the stars sparkled in the clear night sky. I thought again of that desperately poignant scene of a 56 year old father holding his 24 year old dead son's hand and praying at his grave.

As Canon Scott said, it was a miracle that in all the destruction and chaos they were reunited. His words, like the stars, are both matter of fact, and beyond comprehension. As I considered them, the contradiction was too great for my limited mind to grasp. I felt small, forced down by the weight of another human's unbearable experience and the vastness of an existence that the starlight urged me to confront. The monastic night prayer came to mind: "God grant us a quiet night and a perfect end." I said the words aloud, releasing them to the night breeze. I could do no more.

* * *

1. *Dunkirk: Fight to the Last Man*, Hugh Sebag-Montefiore, Penguin 2007, see page 37.
2. A copy of the pardon appears in https://www.executedtoday.com/2009/02/27/1916-james-crozier-an-irishman-in-his-majestys-service/
3. My thanks to Albert's daughter Nen and her husband Bill Billings for their detailed research into Albert Bassett's war record. Unfortunately, much was destroyed by bombing during the Second World War, but War Diaries of the 1/6th Battalion and confirmation of Albert's service were successfully traced at the Public Records Office in Kew. My thanks, too, to Joan Richmond for her memories of Albert after the war.
4. *The History of the Cheshire Regiment in the Great War* by Col. Arthur Crookenden, Naval and Military press, page 71.
5. In May 2018 Chris Morgan and I visited this area again, and managed to locate the trenches that Albert Bassett had served in and the positions of Fort Jackson and Fort Moulin which were about a kilometre apart. There is no sign of them now, but the preserved trenches in Newfoundland Park run right up to the edge of the section of land the Cheshires had occupied. It is possible they might even have been part of it. Standing beside the now gentle grass-covered mounds twisting their way back and forth I pondered the fact that Albert's spade could well have been one of the many that had patched and repaired these enduring witnesses to a world that is now so hard to imagine.
6. "Knife rests" were barbed wire barriers that, in design, called to mind the delicate pieces of tableware upon which a diner could rest their knife during a meal.
7. Order Number 3 written on September 24, 1916 gives reference 39/Maps/M.83. The objective was to "enter the hostile trenches between points Q.17.b.11 & Q.17.b.21". We have a copy of the trench map covering quadrant 17 which shows the German lines, drawn in great detail in red ink bulging out towards the blue British lines which themselves reach out

to their enemy in a "breast-shaped" curve. At the "nipple" there is a point named on the trench maps as "Mary Redan". This is the closest point, where the lines are just a few yards apart.

8. *History of the Cheshire Regiment*, page 88
9. *Ibid* page 96.
10. *Ibid* page 96.
11. *The Great War as I Saw It* by Canon Frederick G Scott CMG, DSO, first published 1922, reprinted in the year 2000 by CEF Books, Ontario, Canada. See pages 100,101, and 106-109 for the account of Henry's death and burial. Quoted with the kind permission of CEF Books.

"Our path took us along a straight, muddy track leading from a farm towards the front lines"

CHAPTER TWELVE

The Mills of God

Albert to Hem-Monacu

Today was a rest day in our schedule but I was keen to keep moving. We were in the October school holidays and the few country buses that existed were on vacation too. So, whilst Fiona caught up on her reading, I decided to take a taxi to the village of Hem-Monacu. From there I would walk back to Albert along a route connecting several battlefield landmarks of the Somme campaign. The distance was about 20km and the taxi driver thought I was daft, but he was too polite to say so directly: "*Vous êtes brave,*" he said.

After a brisk 20 minute drive we reached Hem-Monacu. The taxi dropped me outside the church and disappeared. All was silent. Here on the banks of the Somme river the land fractures into a series of ponds and little islands. Fishermen come with their rod and line to sit and meditate in a landscape designed for contemplation.

Just outside the village, I came to the soldiers' graves at Hem Farm and paused to study the visitors' book. Nearly every Commonwealth War Graves cemetery has one reverently stored with the Cemetery Records in a small chamber, like a tabernacle, built into the brick wall near the entrance. The books are checked regularly to track visitor numbers and help make the case for continuing to fund the care and repair of these sites. Sometimes they contain very personal tributes to a soldier who is buried in the cemetery.

Amongst the pages of Hem Farm's book, I found a bundle of laminated photos left some months before by visiting relatives. One showed a man formally dressed in Salvation Army Uniform and holding a trumpet in his hand. This was Gunner Robert Ralph French who had come all the way from Tasmania to serve with the Australian Field Artillery and to die in action in September 1918 at the age of 32.

Gunner French had kept a diary and in it was a poem which his relatives had copied and added to the photographs. French might have written the poem himself or he might have copied it down from another source. Either way, it was clearly significant to him and I read it carefully:

> *The mills of God grind slowly but they grind exceeding small;*
> *So soft and slow they seem to go they scarcely move at all.*
> *But the souls of men fall into them and are powdered into dust*
> *And in the dust grow sweet white flowers – Love, Hope, and Trust.*[1]

During the Great War, artillery fire literally "ground… the souls of men… into dust" and this experience changed Christians' understanding of a key belief of their faith, the resurrection of the body.

Traditionally, great efforts had been made to bury the dead intact. Writing in 1990, Rev J Aelwyn Roberts recalled that,

> *"In the slate quarry town of Blaenau Ffestiniog, where I was brought up, if a man lost a leg or an arm, or even a finger, in a quarry accident, the cut-off limb would be carefully placed in a little casket and buried in a place apart, in the churchyard, and its place would be marked in the church register. Years later, when Richard Jones or William Davies died of old age his body was laid to rest where the missing limb awaited him. In this way Richard Jones or William Davies could arise whole on the Resurrection Day."* [2]

During the First World War, many thousands of people had been blown into tiny pieces and their relatives would ask the Church, *"What will happen to my loved one on Resurrection Day if he has no body to rise?"* This was a very profound question and theologians struggled to respond to it.

Among them was one who could speak from experience. Fr Pierre Teilhard de Chardin was a French Jesuit priest who had served as a stretcher-bearer in the terrible carnage of Verdun. What Teilhard saw and felt gave him a profound and mystical insight into the nature of reality. Writing to friends from the battlefield he observed that:

> *"Everything that is active, that moves or breathes, every physical, astral or animate energy, every fragment of force, every spark of life, is equally sacred: for, in the humblest atom and the most brilliant star, in the lowest insect and the finest intelligence, there is the radiant smile and thrill of the same absolute."* [3]

Although stretcher-bearers were non-combatants, their role was still extremely dangerous. Teilhard received the Medaille Militaire and France's highest military honour, the Croix de Guerre, for his many acts of courage. When asked why he was so brave, he said simply, *"If I am killed, I shall just change my state, that's all."* [4]

Post-war theologians like Teilhard de Chardin recognised that questions about the Resurrection of the Body were as old as Christianity itself. By moving Christian thinking away from a literal interpretation, they took it back to its origins in Scripture and towards insights which were closer to those that had been so important to Gunner French.

In 1992, the revised Catechism of the Roman Catholic church was finally approved. On the subject of the Resurrection of the Body, it quotes St Paul's guidance to the people of Corinth:

> *"But someone will ask, 'How are the dead raised? With what kind of body do they come?' You foolish man! What you sow does not come to life unless it dies, and what you sow is not the body which is to be, but a bare kernel... What is sown is perishable, what is raised is imperishable... the dead will be raised imperishable...For this perishable nature must put on the imperishable, and this mortal nature must put on immortality.* [5]

* * *

I walked on from Hem-Monacu and found refreshment in a café by the village green in Curlu. From there, I crossed the main road leading back to Albert and reached Maricourt where, in 1916, the British lines had joined those held by the French. When battle began on July 1st the two commanding officers on this section, Lieutenant Colonel Bryan Fairfax and Commandant Le Petit, were the first to leave their trenches. In an astonishing gesture of bravado and solidarity they walked together, hand in hand, in front of their soldiers, leading the attack. Miraculously, both commanders survived the assault and their leadership inspired their troops. On that first disastrous day of the battle of the Somme, this was one of the few areas where British and French forces achieved their objectives.

From Maricourt, my route took me through Carnoy, then back across the main road onto high ground and the Devonshire's trench at Mansel Copse. In preparing for the July battle, Captain Duncan Martin had constructed a contoured plasticine model of this section of the battlefield. Martin was a skilled artist and his model gave an accurate and clear representation of the terrain containing the British and German positions. He showed it to Brigade HQ and drew their attention to the German machine gun that everyone in his unit knew was across the road in Mametz Cemetery. Unless it was put out of action, he predicted, disaster would follow. His advice went unheeded and, on July 1st, Captain Martin and the Devonshires were cut down as soon as they rose up from their trench. The men were all buried where they fell and their bravery is recalled in the words at the entrance to their small cemetery:

"The Devonshires held this trench, and the Devonshires hold it still."

My path continued up the ridge, where it flattened out to loop round behind a wood that overlooks the Devonshires' Cemetery. I had brought copies of World War One trench maps with me [6] so I was able to work out where the lines of the British and German defences had been in the fields ahead. Here, I was following in the footsteps of the poet Siegfried Sassoon on the night he won his Military Cross.

Sassoon had been deeply distressed by the death of a friend and fellow officer, David Thomas. From that moment in March 1916, he nurtured a passion for killing the enemy that made him recklessly brave. His colleagues soon nicknamed him "Mad Jack". When a trench raid was planned for the night of May 25, 1916, Sassoon was disappointed to be only given a backup role. His job was to ensure that the raiders returned safely, so he had to wait on the edge of No Man's Land whilst his unit crept out into the darkness towards the German lines just a 100 yards away. The defenders heard the raiding party approach and as soon as they reached the barbed wire in front of their trench the Germans opened fire. The raid was a complete failure and the raiders hastily withdrew. Several of them were hit and lay in No Man's Land. One of them was Corporal Richard "Mick" O'Brien who, in previous weeks, had gained Sassoon's trust and respect as his partner on several aggressive and dangerous two-man patrols.

Braving enemy fire, Sassoon went out to bring back the wounded. It took him some time to find O'Brien who was in a deep shell crater. He could not be easily reached but, over the next 90 minutes, Sassoon and others worked to rescue their comrade. Respecting their bravery, the Germans held their fire whilst Sassoon used ropes to haul his friend out of the shell crater and then carry him back to the British trench. Sadly, O'Brien did not survive the ordeal, but Sassoon's courage was recognised and he was later decorated.

As the war dragged on, Sassoon became increasingly outspoken in his criticism of the conflict. His anti-war poems became more and more popular but the fact that he had been awarded the Military Cross made it much harder for the authorities to silence him.

Standing where Sassoon had stood, I could once more see, gleaming gold in the sunlight, the statue of the Virgin and Child above the basilica in Albert. Religious themes frequently featured in Sassoon's war poems and, just like Gunner French, he struggled to discern a higher purpose in the frequently terrible experience of daily life. In 1957, Sassoon made what he called his *"unconditional surrender"* in his lifetime's struggle with God. In becoming a Roman Catholic, the man who had once been known as "Mad Jack" found a certainty and happiness he had not known before. *"I am a religious poet,"* he told a friend, a nun at Stanbrook Abbey. [7] Siegfried Sassoon died on September 1st, 1967, just a week short of his 81st birthday.

* * *

1. The opening line is based on the poem *Retribution* by Henry Wadsworth Longfellow.

2. *Holy Ghostbuster – A Parson's Encounters with the Paranormal* by Rev J Aelwyn Roberts, Element books 1996. Despite its title, this is a thoughtful record of ghosts and spirits encountered during Roberts' 36 years as Vicar of Llandegai in North Wales. He died in January 2018, aged 99.

3. Page 28 of the essay *Cosmic Life* written in 1916 and published by Harper & Row in *Writings in Time of War* by Pierre Tielhard de Chardin, translated by René Hague. Now available on-line https://archive.org/details/WritingsInTimeOfWar/page/n25/mode/2up

4. https://teilhard.com/life-of-teilhard-de-chardin/war-years-1914-1918-finding-god-in-suffering .

5. *First letter of St Paul to the Corinthians*, Chapter 15, verse 35 onwards. http://vatican.va/archive/ENG0015/_P2H.HTM

6. Published in *The Somme Battlefield* by Ruaraidh Adams-Cairns, Hayloft Publishing 2014.

7. Page 71, *Anthem for Doomed Youth – 12 Soldier Poets of the First World War* by Jon Stallworthy, Constable 2005. Corporal Richard "Mick" O'Brien is buried in Citadel New Military Cemetery, close to where he died.

"The Devonshires held this trench, and the Devonshires hold it still"

CHAPTER THIRTEEN

St Fursey

Péronne, Clastres

Thus far, every yard of the walk from Dunkirk had contained countless stories and reminders of the wars our parents and grandparents knew so well. English speaking writers have researched these places so thoroughly that it would be easy to conclude that the First World War of 1914–18 was only about the British Empire's battle with Germany. However, the Somme valley marks a turning point where the British story begins to diminish and the far greater French story begins to unfold. From here, the front lines that were held almost exclusively by French troops twist on for another 350 miles or so (three times the distance from Nieuport) before finishing on the Swiss border at the hamlet of Mooselargue. Our path would now take us back and forth across these French and German lines until, at Reims, the old battlefront would continue due east whilst we would continue south.

This is also the point where our journey to Rome connected once more with the route followed by Sigeric in AD 990. Alison Raju's excellent pocket guide to the Via Francigena could now replace the detailed IGN maps that had guided us so well on the Somme battlefields.

A taxi took us from Albert to Hem-Monacu from where our path led us through Herbécourt and on to re-join the Via Francigena at Péronne. Péronne is an ancient town built on a hill that dominates the Somme river and lakes. It has seen many invading armies and photos in the town's cafes recall its occupation by the Germans in 1914. Today, Péronne's centre is dominated by a great fortified château with high stone walls and rounded towers. It has the look of an English castle but, inside, an excellent museum tells the story of the Great War from the French perspective.

The Franco-Prussian War of 1870–71 had been a bitter defeat for France. Territory was lost, Paris itself captured and the nation humiliated. The experience was still fresh in living memory when, in 1914, von Moltke's troops swept down from the north and once more threatened the capital. By September, the situation was so desperate that taxi-cabs drove out from Paris to provide transport for General Joffre's regiments in their last-ditch effort to hold the advancing enemy at the River Marne. Joffre's strategy was successful and he was hailed as France's saviour. The rapid movement of armies ended, the troops dug their trenches and the static war settled into its pattern of attrition. The four years of conflict took a heavy toll on France. At Verdun, the French army bled dry and, after the disaster on the Chemin des Dames in 1917, it refused to fight on. By the time the Armistice was signed in November 1918, an estimated 5.5 million French soldiers had been killed or wounded compared to an estimated 2.5 million troops from the United Kingdom.[1] The nation had barely recovered from the trauma when Hitler's armies threatened again in 1939.

∗ ∗ ∗

One positive consequence of the German invasion of 1914 was that it prompted the French state and the Roman Catholic church to reconcile their differences. For decades, state legislation had sought to curtail the Church's influence. In some cases, this had led to the confiscation of church assets and the exiling of its clergy. For example, in 1903 armed soldiers seized the famous Cistercian Abbey of Grande Chartreuse and sent the monks into exile. The Abbey was handed over to businessmen who planned to acquire production of the world famous and very lucrative Chartreuse liquor. However, the canny monks took their secret with them to Catalonia and the bogus business failed.

In 1914, Church and State put their differences aside to share a common purpose and resist this new invasion. Catholics could now, in good conscience, serve their country. A total of 12,305 clergy and religious went on to be decorated for their service at the battlefront, 4,820 of them dying *Mort pour La France*.[2]

Many, like Fr Pierre Teilhard de Chardin, served in non-combatant roles. However, the former seminarian Léon Bourjade brought his Catholic faith with him into combat as a fighter pilot. Whilst studying for the priesthood, Bourjade became devoted to Thérèse of Lisieux. Thérèse was a young Carmelite nun who had sought sanctity by performing small, apparently insignificant acts of love. Her spiritual memoir was published after she died from tuberculosis at the age of 24. Thérèse's "Little Way" of holiness became very popular, especially with ordinary people who could relate to her search for the sacred in the small things of everyday life. After her death in 1897, Thérèse's reputation grew and, in June 1914, Pope Pius X opened the case for her formal canonisation. However, for many people "The Little Flower", as she was known, was already a saint.

When, in 1917, Léon Bourjade joined the pilots of *L'escadrille 152* he decided to invoke Thérèse's blessing by painting her portrait on the side of his single seat SPAD fighter. Bourjade became expert in attacking enemy observation balloons. These floating aerial platforms enabled observers to spy behind their enemy's front lines and accurately guide artillery fire onto their targets. They posed a huge threat and destroying them was a top priority. However, although the balloons looked vulnerable, they were heavily defended by anti-aircraft guns and lurking fighter patrols. Attacking them was a very dangerous business. Despite these risks, Bourjade was extremely successful. He shot down a total of 27 balloons and was awarded the Légion d'Honneur for his courage. Some of the German observers Bourjade attacked would also have been devout Catholics. What they thought as they saw "The Little Flower" swooping towards them, machine guns blazing fire and death, is not recorded.[3]

* * *

Fiona and I had booked a small apartment overlooking Péronne's main square. Opposite was the huge church of St John the Baptist where, for over 1,200 years, pilgrims had come to venerate the bones of St Fursey.

By all accounts, Fursey (or Fursa) was a remarkable man. Born around AD 597, his missionary work took him from his birthplace near Connacht in Ireland, across to East Anglia and then to France. The Venerable Bede wrote extensively of his outstanding goodness, his visions of the unseen world of good and evil spirits and of the afterlife. Fursey would fall into long, trance-like states during which he would describe scenes of the fires of falsehood, covetousness, discord and injustice which were lying in wait to consume the world. This was a terrible gift for Fursey to live with. One witness described how, during one of his visions,

"although it was during a time of severe winter weather and a hard frost and though Fursa sat wearing only a thin garment, yet as he told his story, he sweated as though it were in the middle of summer, either because of the terror or else the joy which his recollections aroused." [1]

Centuries later, St Fursey's visions would continue to influence Western European religious thought. Dante's *Divine Comedy* completed in 1320, is believed to have been inspired by Fursey's experiences.

Fursey impressed everyone who met him. So many miracles were attributed to him in his own lifetime that he was counted among the greatest of saints. On his arrival in France, Fursey restored to life the son of a local nobleman, Count Haymon. The Count begged Fursey to build his monastery on land he owned at Mezerolles, but Fursey declined. However, when Fursey died at Mezerolles around 650 it seemed that the Count would have his wish fulfilled. However, Fursey's sanctity was so well known that French kings and nobles vied with each other to possess his remains. Count Haymon's plans to inter Fursey in Mezerolles were thwarted by the Chancellor of Péronne, Erchinoald, who sent a royal guard to seize Fursey's body and bring it to the town. As soon as they arrived,

Fursey's remains became a focus for pilgrimage and they continued to attract pilgrims from all stations of life for centuries to come. King Louis IX was among them. Returning from the crusades in 1256, the King declared that he wished to be present for the retranslation of St Fursey's remains to a new shrine in the church. When all was done, King Louis placed his seal on the new sepulchre and here St Fursey's bones remained until the Great War brought an end to his peaceful rest.

In July 1918, Allied troops advanced on German occupied Péronne. Heavy shellfire landed near the church, shattering stained glass windows and statues. The parish priest, Abbe Dubois, decided to abandon the building but first he knew he must protect St Fursey's relics. Hurriedly removing Fursey's bones from the shrine, the priest took them to the most secure place he knew, the safe in the sacristy where the valuable silver chalices were kept. This would be strong enough to protect the precious relics even if the whole church was destroyed around it. More shells were exploding nearby, and Abbe Dubois had to hurry. However, in his panic he made a crucial mistake. A leaflet in the church tells visitors *"Trusting in human nature, Abbe Dubois leaves the key in the lock."* When the priest returned, the relics were gone. They have never been seen again.[5]

* * *

Sadly, for a place with such a long history of pilgrimage, the Church of St John the Baptist did not appear to acknowledge its place on the Via Francigena. There were no welcoming signs and no one who could stamp our pilgrim passports. We went to the Tourist Office nearby where a friendly woman was happy to provide us with a record of our visit. Unfortunately, the only stamp she had was a rather disappointing celebration of the tourist office itself.

The small villages of Cartigny, Trefcon and Etreillers we now passed through seemed as uninterested as Péronne in being part of the Via Francigena. Churches remained locked and only the face of Pope Francis smiling out from posters on church noticeboards cheered us on our way.

The posters promoted "evangelism" but, looking at these depressed, silent buildings festooned with bird droppings, it seemed a lost cause. Still, if anyone could inspire evangelism, Francis could. Even these small images of him brought a glimmer of hope and energy.

A big notice at Seraucourt-le-Grand proclaimed that this had been Archbishop Sigeric's 73rd overnight stop from Rome and we marked it by sitting beside a pleasant lake to eat our sandwiches. Leaving the village, the road took us through open fields as they climbed up a ridge towards four wind turbines turning lazily in the breeze. We could hear a rasping buzzing noise coming from their direction and we wondered what was ahead.

The turbines stood on the outskirts of the old airfield at Clastres, but the buzzing that we heard was not the ghostly whirr of aero engines. Beyond the perimeter fence, a string of trials bikes revved around a prepared track. Speeding up as they approached a ramp, each took to the air in spectacular fashion before landing firmly on both wheels and driving on. We stood and watched and admired their skill.

Beyond the airfield, we could see Clastres church with the sunlight shining through its distinctive lattice spire. Clastres would mark the end of our daily walking. We'd calculated that we did not have enough time left to walk the remaining 57 kilometres to Laon and give that fascinating city the attention it deserved. The prospect of an overnight stay in the railway junction at Tergnier didn't inspire either. The guidebook's description of it as *a sort of French version of Crewe* seemed, however unfairly, to say it all so, instead, we'd arranged to meet up with our friends Chris and Chris. They were now on their way from Kent and we had a couple of hours before they were due to arrive at Clastres and drive us the final stage to Laon. The guidebook promised a café in the village and afternoon tea beckoned. The future looked good.

Alas, the café had closed down long ago and Clastres itself was deserted apart from a group of bored teenagers wandering up and down the empty street. All the welcome that the village had to offer was a *defibrillateur* securely fastened to the wall of the Mairie. Fine, if you were dying from a heart attack, but not much use if you were suffering from dehydration, incontinence or just plain loneliness.

We sat on a seat beside the locked church and settled down to wait. A memorial on the wall of the cemetery behind us remembered all those who had served at the aerodrome during the Second World War. It was a complex history. Erected in 2001, the memorial recalled how, between 1939 and 1945, French, then German and finally American squadrons had operated from Clastres airfield. Interestingly, all were acknowledged equally, friend and foe alike. French Potez aircraft and American Marauders and Lightnings were given tribute alongside Messerschmitt 109s and Focke-Wulf 190s. Brought up on more partisan narratives of war, I found it strange to see friend and foe celebrated together on one memorial, each unit asking in their own language not to be forgotten.

The churchyard itself was raised up on a mound behind the wall. Here was Clastres' history, fading and crumbling. Amongst the crucifixes, I found a small obelisk belonging to the Joly Dufetel family. One of its inscriptions was dedicated to Jean-Marie Joly *du 2eme cuirassiers, tué a Waterloo*. Here in Clastres, we were reminded of that great battle of June 1815 when British and Prussian forces united to thwart French ambitions. Such is the changing nature of alliances in European history.

Anglo-French rivalries are long and deep rooted. In 1889, the British were still building forts on the North Downs ridge in Surrey to protect London from a possible French invasion. Even when the British army's professional soldiers arrived on the continent in August 1914, many thought it strange that they were coming to fight the Germans, not the French. We realised how blessed we are to enjoy this time of peace, but history reminds us that it is fragile. To survive, it needs to be guarded, cared for and renewed.

* * *

1. https://en.wikipedia.org/wiki/World_War_I_casualties. Germany lost around 6 million and Austria-Hungary around five million military killed or wounded.
2. Quoted in display notes in Verdun Cathedral's special exhibition (2016) on the Catholic Church and the Great War
3. https://en.wikipedia.org/wiki/L%C3%A9on_Bourjade. Léon Bourjade survived the war and was ordained a priest in 1921. He joined the Sacred Heart Missionaries in Papua New Guinea where he died in 1924 at the age of 35.
4. This account by the Venerable Bede is quoted in *Beda* by Henrietta Leyser, published by Head of Zeus, 2015, page 140.
5. An ecumenical group of devotees to St Fursey, www.furseypilgrims.co.uk are focused around Burgh Castle near Great Yarmouth in Norfolk where tradition places St Fursey's original monastery. Their research reports that some relics of St Fursey from Péronne are now kept in St John the Baptist Church in Lagny-sur-Marne, east of Paris, but there is no mention of this in the leaflet in St Fursey's chapel in Péronne.

Clastres church

CHAPTER FOURTEEN

A Pilgrim's Welcome

Laon

Our lengthy stay in Clastres was becoming tedious. We'd begun to consider testing the *defibrillateur* just for entertainment's sake when, soon after 5 pm, Chris and Chris drove into the square as planned. It was Thursday evening, and the remaining kilometres to the mysterious town of Laon were quickly covered.

The ancient town of Laon hovers like a spaceship over the flat planes of Picardy. Floating on a rocky outcrop 100 metres above the ground, its great cathedral draws the traveller towards its mystery.

We booked into the delightful Hotel des Arts next to the railway station. From the balcony of our first-floor room we could look over the rooftops to the two kilometre long, 400-metre wide ridge upon which the historic old town stood, crowned by the great Cathedral of Notre Dame de Laon.

From the train station, a small automatic funicular railway took us to the top of the plateau. Here we entered a medieval world of ancient buildings and archways, narrow cobbled lanes and convivial squares. From the town's walls, the view was breath-taking. Green fields and dark woods stretched out to the far horizon whilst, below, the railway with its station were laid out like a child's toy train set.

Once the centre of power for Carolingian kings, Laon was, in the 11th and 12th centuries, the seat of Europe's most famous school of theology and biblical scholarship under Anselm of Laon. The town's immense wealth and prestige at that time provided both the means and the ambition to create a wonder of the age. Notre Dame de Laon was one of the first cathedrals to be built in the new Gothic style, using innovative engineering techniques to create a vast sacred space filled with light and colour.

Around the deep porches of the three west doors, a crowd of sculpted life-size figures stood just a few feet above the ground. Each one's character was clear to see and it was as if they were welcoming us personally. Above them, two of the cathedral's towers soared upwards into the air. Huge oxen looked down from their high altitude arcades, horned beasts that, depending on your frame of mind, could appear benign or demonic. This abundance of detail was overwhelming and almost too much to take in. Yet, what was even more astonishing was the fact that there were hardly any other people around. It was as if we were the first to discover this awesome building and receive its intimate welcome. In the absence of the usual crowds of tourist visitors, we had this wonderful place to ourselves.[1]

Despite its spectacular setting, its richness of architecture and its depth of history, Laon is in an impoverished part of France. During our walk along the Via Francigena, we had met several people who had told us we were heading for a poor area, where unemployment was high and far right political parties were strong. On closer inspection, we could see that many of the ancient buildings did indeed seem to be crumbling and even parts of the cathedral were in desperate need of repair.

Laon is now more a provincial town with a great history than a city with a thriving economy. During the First War, Laon had been far behind the German lines. Safe from bombardment, the Cathedral had served as a hospital and filled its aisles with beds for sick and wounded soldiers. During the Second War, Allied aircraft bombed parts of the town but thankfully nearly all the wonderful medieval architecture survived. From here, it is just a short drive to the infamous 1917 battlefields of the Chemin des Dames where inept leadership and more terrible slaughter resulted in mutiny amongst many French army units. Laon is therefore a natural base for exploring this phase of the Great War yet, for whatever reason, the tourists do not gather here in great numbers. Nor do many pilgrims, although there is plenty that should draw them to this the 72nd stage in Sigeric's journey.

That said, what is bad news for the people who have to make a living in Laon is good news for the adventurous traveller. Notre Dame de Laon, with its original 12th century stained-glass windows and equally old and mysterious icon of the Holy Face of Laon, must be the only ancient cathedral where, at certain times of the day, you can find yourself completely, wonderfully alone.

* * *

My hopes of attending Mass in the cathedral were to be disappointed. Although we'd arrived in Laon on Thursday evening, there was no Mass in the cathedral until 11 am on Sunday, by which time we would be on our way back to the Eurotunnel at Calais. Fortunately, another of Laon's great churches, St Martin's, had Mass at 6 pm on Saturday evening so I set off to find it at the other end of the plateau.

The Abbey of St Martin was founded in 1124 as one of the earliest Premonstratensian communities. When the French Revolution dissolved the Abbey, its church survived and continues to be the focus of an active parish. Beside it, Laon's modern hospital still provides the medical care that was once such an important part of the monastic way of life.

Although the Premonstratensians had almost disappeared by the start of the 19th century, they have since enjoyed a steady revival. Now known as the Norbertines (St Norbert had founded the order in a rural place called Prémontré, hence their original name) they have nearly 100 communities across the world. Sadly, there is not one in Laon but I was delighted to discover that I'd been helping to fund them on this journey. One of their sources of income comes from brewery deals for Leffe and Grimbergen beers.

I entered St Martin's through its west door and found about 200 people already gathered for Mass. Looking up, I admired the high, snow white stone vaulted roof above me and the white stone pillars running along each side of the nave. In contrast, dark wood panels on the walls and the dark wood of the altar itself warmed the atmosphere. In the evening light, the overall effect was both inviting and welcoming.

It was a beautiful service. An elderly woman skilfully played a Spanish guitar and the congregation confidently sang the hymns. Together, we did justice to the wonderful acoustic qualities of the church itself. My French was not good enough to follow the sermon but I did recognise the Gospel account from Matthew in which Jesus is asked to decide which one of the Ten Commandments is the greatest. I remembered that I had studied this text a couple of weeks before as I prepared to write my reflection for our own parish newsletter. Sitting there in Laon, I realised that parishioners of St Anselm's, Tooting Bec were now reading my words at their own evening Mass in London. Like those of us here, they too would be pondering the implications of Jesus' summary of the Law for their own lives.

"You must love the Lord your God with all your heart, with all your soul and with all your mind…and you must love your neighbour as yourself." [2]

After the Consecration, the elderly priest invited the children to gather around the altar to say the Our Father together. About 20 did so and it was nice to watch their curious little faces as they said their prayers and followed the priest's gentle and patient guidance. When the congregation were invited to share together a sign of peace, we turned to those beside us and shook hands. I was near the front and at the end of a pew by the centre aisle. A little boy, aged about four and wearing big round glasses, left the altar, walked down the aisle and stopped beside my pew. His face was stern as he stretched his hand out towards me. He was on an important mission. I shook his hand and bowed slightly. The young ambassador for peace turned and moved on, keeping his solemn expression as he shook the hand of the person in the pew behind me. It was a moment of pure delight.

At St Martin's, I had not spoken to anyone personally, but I had felt part of a community of people, young and old, who were enjoying being there together. Walking back, I followed a cobblestone path tracing the southern edge of the plateau as it curved gently away in front of me. The view ahead was majestic and wonderful. As the sky darkened into night, the floodlit Cathedral of Our Lady of Laon seemed to float above the rooftops, a witness to sacred mysteries far beyond our limited comprehension, yet which, that evening, had been illuminated by a young child's solemn, reverent gesture of welcome to a visiting pilgrim.

* * *

1. There is a thread that links the start of our journey with this chapter's end. During his exile from England, Thomas Becket came to visit Laon in 1164 and one of the cathedral's five great towers is named after him.
2. *Gospel of Matthew*, 22: verses 37–40.

"The Cathedral of Our Lady of Laon seemed to float above the rooftops"

Postscript

Since those first notes were written in a Balham café in 2013, I've realised that I am on three simultaneous journeys. The first, of course, is the walk itself and, as I write, Fiona and I have reached Vercelli in Northern Italy. We have crossed the Alps and descended through the beautiful Aosta valley to Anselm's birth place and beyond to "the rice capital of Europe." Next year, we plan to follow the footpaths from Vercelli along the edges of Italy's rice fields before they take us on across the Appenines and into Tuscany.

Planning for the next stage is the second journey. During this, I live in the future, imagining it, calculating it stage by stage, day by day. With luck, from Vercelli we will reach Pontremoli where we will be just 493 kilometres from Rome.

Then there is the third journey, the written one, relived at my computer. I read my diaries, research the places we have visited and learn more about the lives of people who have gone before us on this journey. In the meantime, ordinary life goes on, weaving its way between the three.

Fr Gerry W. Hughes passed away in 2014 and his final book, *Cry of Wonder*, was published just before he died. He had reached the age of 90 and, even though he could no longer manage more than a few steps, he was still known as Fr Gerry "The Walk" Hughes. Happily, his mind was clear and active to the end and he continued to write with insight and compassion.

A good friend also passed away at the beginning of this year. Fiona's mum and Albert Bassett's daughter, Joan Richmond, died suddenly just a couple of weeks before her 91st birthday. Like Fr Gerry's, her body had become frailer, but her mind was sharp and her life was full of friends and laughter. Christmas had been a typically joyful, rumbustious family occasion and she was still enjoying the memory of it when, whilst waiting for her evening meal to cook, a heart attack took her in a second.

What is it like to die? Just a few days before Joan's death, an elderly friend, Anne Walsh, had told me of her experience in surviving a stroke which, in other circumstances, would have ended her life. Anne had made an excellent recovery and one day when we'd met for coffee after Mass at St Anselm's she told me what had happened:

"I was at Mass when I collapsed. I remember feeling myself go and putting my hand out behind me to try to steady myself against a pillar. My next memory was waking up in hospital five hours later. They'd used a new procedure to remove the blood clot. To be successful, this procedure had to be done within the first six hours of the stroke happening. I'm so lucky that people called an ambulance straight away and that I was so close to one of the best hospitals in the country. In other circumstances, I would have died."

"So, what did it feel like?" I asked. *"Dying, I mean?"*

"It was very peaceful," Anne replied. *"That's what I remember, just how peaceful it was."*

Anne's experience gave us great comfort when Joan died. We were reassured that she had not suffered. In Fr Pierre Tielhard de Chardin's words, Joan had just changed her state, that's all.

We held the wake in a pub, the Rose of York, below the Petersham Hotel on Richmond Hill. We couldn't afford the Hotel, but the Rose of York was close to it. This was important, as the Petersham Hotel was one of Joan's favourite places. Its stunning view from Richmond Hill looks down on the river Thames as it curves through Petersham and Ham fields on its way to Hampton Court and Windsor. It is a remarkable landscape where the countryside holds its ground, charming and defiant against further urban encroachment.

Some years ago, the five of us, Joan, Fiona, our sons Tom, Sam and myself, were sat together in the Petersham Hotel's restaurant looking out across the river. Joan and Fiona both agreed that this view was one of their most favourite places and we asked the boys what were theirs. Interestingly, both took their minds back to happy childhood family moments. Tom recalled the view from a high point in the hills above Betws-y-Coed in North Wales from where we could look down onto Elsie Lake. After a tough walk up and out of the valley we had paused to admire the lake shining like a mirror far below and to look in wonder at the spectacular Snowdon mountains revealed in the distance. Disney's cartoon film *The Lion King* was popular at the time and we named the spot where we stood "Pride Rock". It has been remembered so ever since.

We wondered what place Sam would choose as his favourite and, not surprisingly, football came to his mind. *"Fratton Park,"* he said, *"particularly that patch of grass by the corner flag to the right, looking out from the Milton End."* "Why there?" we asked. *"That's where we saw LuaLua do his back somersault after he'd scored for Portsmouth. He was right in front of us."* Sam and I have followed Portsmouth for many years and goals were rare in their Premier League days. Lomana LuaLua's athleticism and sheer joy in his trade mark celebration had indeed made the moment wondrous.

Pilgrim routes and religious shrines are made sacred not only by the lives and experiences of those they commemorate, but also by the prayers of those who come in search of them. These are the "thin places" that Celtic spirituality speaks of, where time is transcended and the boundary between heaven and earth seems almost to dissolve. In whatever way we understand such words, these places open us to encounter the mystery of God.

Richmond Hill, North Wales and Fratton Park may not be considered religious settings, but, infused with memories of deep love and joy, they form part of the holy ground that is within us, the very ground of our being.

Fr Gerry knew that *Cry of Wonder* would be his final book. In its Preamble, he tried to explain his purpose in writing it:

> "*I write about this in order to encourage the reader to value and cherish their own experience... to discover the treasure, the pearl of great price, which is on offer to you... simply because you are a human being called to play a unique role in creation and be at one with that power which Dante writes of, the power 'that moves the sun and other stars,' the power of Love. This power is nearer to each one of us than we are to ourselves.*"[1]

It is the love we share with others, especially those closest to us, that endures. The pilgrim journey helps by giving us perspective. It can sharpen into focus the treasure that has become blurred by its closeness to us. When the walking is over, what we return to and bring back with us is what counts the most. Holy ground is created when it is tilled by deep love, sometimes in great deeds, heroic or tragic, sometimes in struggle, sometimes in peace. Most times it is in the small and the ordinary, the mundane acts of daily life. The secret is that this holy ground is recognised and appreciated, so it can nourish us for the next stage of our journey.

* * *

1. © Gerard W Hughes, 2014, *Cry of Wonder*, Continuum Publishing, used by permission of Bloomsbury Publishing plc pages x, xi.

Joan with her five grandchildren, Christmas 2016